MARRIAGE AND THE FAMILY UNDER CHALLENGE

AN OUTLINE OF ISSUES, TRENDS, AND ALTERNATIVES

DOROTHY FAHS BECK

ANNOTATED BIBLIOGRAPHY
EMILY BRADSHAW

Second Edition

FAMILY SERVICE ASSOCIATION OF AMERICA
NEW YORK

First edition, *Current Challenges to the Traditional Family and Some Newly Emerging Alternate Forms for Family Living*,

International Standard Book Number: 0-87304-145-3
Library of Congress Catalog Card Number: 76-26307

Printed in the United States of America

CONTENTS

INTRODUCTORY NOTES

PURPOSE

The outline format and annotated bibliography are designed to provide a convenient overview of the multifaceted challenges to marriage and the family and to indicate at a glance the diversity of proposals and experiments for their revitalization. This review was undertaken in response to numerous requests and expressions of interest and concern. Its content is based principally on the writing and research of persons not on the staffs of family service agencies, particularly social scientists, whose many contributions to the literature FSAA acknowledges with much appreciation.

Because of the rapidity of recent changes, the information available is still scattered, fragmentary, and only sparsely documented. At this time little reliable data are available either on the total prevalence of these new family life-styles and related attitudes or on their variation by region, race and ethnic group, or socioeconomic status. Neither is current information sufficient to permit a sound evaluation of their long-term potential advantages or dangers. What is abundantly clear, however, is that common human problems and needs are reappearing under new guises and may require new approaches in service. A necessary prelude to the design of relevant and effective services to meet these needs is further knowledge about these experiments and challenges. Also required is the initiation of direct contact and active engagement with those involved in this search for new and more fulfilling patterns in human relationships. This review represents a beginning effort to facilitate this type of outreach.

SOURCES

This summary was originally prepared in outline form for use in informal talks. Because of widespread interest, it has been revised and updated for a wider audience. The following sources have been used in its preparation: (1) selected books and periodicals, (2) papers and discussions at conferences, and (3) informal exchanges with agency staff, family, and friends. The supporting materials have been selected to be representative rather than comprehensive.

REFERENCE CITATIONS

Reference numbers in the text that are enclosed in parentheses refer to the accompanying bibliography prepared by Emily Bradshaw, FSAA Director of Information Services. These citations are intended to be suggestive rather than inclusive and cover only selected items in the outline. General topics discussed in the majority of the references are not supported with citations. References cited in footnote form as superscripts refer to the footnotes listed on pages 42-46. They indicate the specific source of the statistics or quotation cited.

OUTLINE OF ISSUES, TRENDS, AND ALTERNATIVES

BY

DOROTHY FAHS BECK

I. CHALLENGES TO MARRIAGE AND THE FAMILY

A. Some indicators of the seriousness of the current challenge

Lederer and Jackson affirm that the "state of marriage is a calamity."[1]
The New York Times Magazine of August 15, 1971, carries a cover picture showing the nuclear family as an antique curiosity exhibited under a glass bell.
Cooper titles his provocative book *The Death of the Family*. (21)
Cadwallader calls contemporary marriage "a wretched institution."[2]

B. Aspects of marriage and the family being challenged

1. <u>Nature of courtship</u>

Criticism of traditional courtship as not being a realistic preparation for marriage
Dating more informal
Dating not limited to male initiative; expenses often shared
Passing of chaperonage
More open and earlier sexual orientation and stimulation
Bypassing of formal engagements
Redefinition of engagement
Challenge to concept of romantic love (11, 22, 26)

Reduction in pressure to marry; push for acceptable alternatives
Refusal of universities to continue *in loco parentis* role
Widespread use of co-ed dorms (see V-A)
Living with opposite sex in fraternities, dorms, and apartments (see V-A)
Increase in premarital sex, especially among women (4, 49, 89)[3]
Increased housing provision for free-floating relationships between singles--singles clubs, luxury apartments for singles with recreational facilities, apartments for "swingers" (10; 89, p. 209)
Rapid, informal progress toward intimacy

2. When to marry

Push for delay in commitment
Resistance to legal ties
Argument that marriage is unnecessary unless there are children

3. Whether to marry at all

Criticisms: Marriage is obsolete. Family is too limiting. Family unit should be larger. New forms for intimate relationships are needed.
Singlehood should be a fully acceptable life-style alternative. (1, 57, 113)

4. Type of marriage

Serial monogamy (3, 119)
Probationary marriage (119)

Definition of early phase of marriage as an "apprentice period" (103)
Renewable contract (26, 103)
Two-year confirmation period (89, pp. 466-68)
Two types--individual marriage, parental marriage (75)
Limitation of formalized marriages to couples planning to have children (40)
Making marriage a nonlegal voluntary association (40)

5. Who should marry whom

One man, one woman
Two men
Two women
Same sex marriages with one partner's sex identity shifted (transvestism)
Multilateral marriages
Whole communities--communes

6. Nature of marriage ceremony
(40; 99, p. 26)

Tendency of many to omit religious ceremony, legal ceremony, or both
Change in content of ceremonies (for example, omission of religious references, omission of promises of "till death do us part")
Ceremonial forms: numerous, varied (for example, writing own ceremonies, double rings, no rings), exotic (in location, timing, dress)

7. How wife should be addressed

Keeping own family name
Hyphenating own name and husband's family name
Choosing entirely new name

Objections to use of Miss and Mrs.; Ms. preferred

8. Duration of marriage

Questioning of lifetime monogamy
Open-ended pair bonding, not permanency, seen as goal
Stress on self-expression, personal needs; hedonistic flavor

9. How marriage should be terminated

Recommended elimination of court procedures built on adversary roles, fault allocated to one person, and public display of bitterness
Questioning of alimony--required only in some circumstances, should sometimes go to man, equal division of property as an alternative
Recommended changes in insurance provisions to provide for divorce--for example, divorce insurance, change in social security laws so that wife can carry share of husband's benefits with her when divorcing

10. Extent to which sexual exclusivity is essential within marriage

Increasing openness about infidelity within marriage, plus increasing challenge of "double standard" on fidelity (35, 48, 49, 57, 66, 74, 80, 83, 94, 95, 109, 115, 117, 118)
Alternate models: commitment with exclusivity, commitment without exclusivity, neither

Search for varietism, plus search for more depth in relationship
Programmed provision for varietism: individual mate swapping, organized swinging, open marriage, alternative marriage models, sexual freedom generally

11. <u>Permissible types of sexual stimulation</u>

Changing standards on pornography and nudity (33, 49, 57)
More open sexual titillation on stage, in movies, in mass media, in peep shows
Pressures for removal of legal controls of deviant sexual practices between consenting adults
Decline in guilt feelings about deviant forms of sexuality and autoerotic behavior (49)

12. <u>How families are housed</u>

Criticism that separate houses or apartments for each family are inefficient
Recommendation that apartment buildings provide facilities for communal eating, child care, household services, and recreation (116)
Recommendation that major capital assets, such as cars, be shared by more than one family
Recommendation that spouses not necessarily be expected to live together or with their children (23)

13. <u>Expectations of marriage</u>

Higher expectations regarding depth

of relating, communication, intimacy, sexual relationships, and equity

Lower expectations in regard to family's providing the major source of security because of women's working and social security protections

Increased use of husband-wife advance contracts covering their exchange agreements (34, 123)

14. <u>Family role patterns</u>

Blurring of sexually distinct roles within and outside the home--fuller sharing of household tasks, part-time jobs for both men and women (7, 8, 12, 117, 118)

More sharing in control of money

Widespread challenge to traditional power structure and ways of making family decisions, such as those regarding moving

Bernard's criticism that "marriage is a poor status for women" (7)

Push for extension of family boundaries to include intimate contacts within a wider network (55, 94, 95, 114; see also II-C)

15. <u>Fertility control and limitations</u>

Increasing variety of approaches: regular pill, morning-after pill, long-lasting injections, experiments with vaginal suppository (for abortions)

Increasing availability of information on contraception

Legalization of abortion

Challenge as to which sex should

carry burden of fertility control; increase in discussion and prevalence of vasectomy as an option

Criticism of large families as unethical (Ideal family size is also reported declining.)

Questions by some about desirability of having children at all (see V-C)

Suggestion that only those licensed by the state be permitted to have children (26)

16. <u>How children should be conceived</u>

Opening up of a wider choice of biological father (for example, through artificial insemination, sperm banks) (119)

Sex of child now partially controllable

Genetic counseling (plus medical diagnostic tests) increasingly promoting selective termination of pregnancy

17. <u>How children should be born</u> (61)

Movement toward natural childbirth

Movement toward return of delivery process to the home

Provision for closer, more natural mother-child contact in hospital

Increased provision for husband to be present during delivery

Rejection by some of legal registration of births

18. <u>How children should be reared</u>

Push for increased sharing of child-rearing role by both partners (8; see also I-B-14)

Experimentation with communal child rearing (assumption of parental responsibility by total community) (31, 47, 50, 55, 101, 108, 118)

Increase in day care facilities

Increase in single persons' electing parenthood by choice (see V-B)

Proposed substitutes for child rearing by biological parents (23, 64, 119)

Withholding of some children entirely from public schools and substitution of education at home

Criticism of heavy achievement pressures characteristic of middle-class parents (total permissiveness encouraged by some communes)

Avoidance of sex stereotyping in child rearing

19. <u>How the aged are cared for</u>

Less inclusion of elderly parents in the households of children (except for certain minority groups)

Increase in care of older persons outside the homes of their children; rapid expansion of special communities for the aged and nursing homes

Discussion of experiments with group living for the aged (14, 115, 119)

Proposal that polygamy may serve the needs of persons over sixty (14, 53, 86, 98, 119)

20. <u>How the nuclear family relates to the extended family</u>
(38, 55, 114, 116)

More living alone or in small family units rather than with relatives
Increased intergenerational communication barriers; more distance and fewer contacts

II. RECENT COUNTERMOVEMENTS DESIGNED TO REVITALIZE FAMILY LIVING

A. Efforts to revitalize marriage (70, 71, 79, 83, 86, 87, 88)

Rapid expansion of a variety of models for group experiences focused on marriage enrichment
Improvement of preparation for marriage: school instruction in marriage and family development, home economics, and sex education; premarital groups for engaged couples
Development and improved availability and specificity of professional help with the sexual problems of couples (new sex therapies)
Development of a variety of methods for group training of couples in improved communcation
Emphasis on growth model rather than medical pathology model in describing marital relationships--for example, expansion of human potential movement
Development of national organizations to support this effort (Association of Couples for Marriage Enrichment, Council of Affiliated Marriage Enrichment Organizations)

B. Efforts to improve child-rearing patterns (79, 86, 87)

Expansion of training for parenthood and family life generally

Development of specific techniques for improving coping skills of parents (for example, Parent Effectiveness Training, Filial Therapy Program, Parent Adolescent Relationship Program, social learning approach)

C. Efforts to promote greater intimacy between families

Family cluster movement (92), family networks (55, 86, 114)

Family camping experiments (87)

Expansion of therapeutic approaches to include multiple families (for example, couples' groups, multiple-family therapy, network therapy)

D. Efforts to revitalize the older years

Growing opposition to fixed age cutoff points for retirement and for career changes

Efforts to resist negative stereotyping of aged and assumption that attenuated satisfactions and deterioration are necessarily characteristic of the older years

Efforts to help the older person cope with problems inherent in enforced leisure, low income, poor health, loneliness; preretirement and postretirement educational programs

Efforts to upgrade nursing home care and reduce exploitation

Beginning of attention to the special problems of the aged in disadvantaged groups

III. DOCUMENTATION OF CHANGES IN MARRIAGE AND THE FAMILY
(9, 10, 32, 38, 49)

A. Statistics reflecting the increased frequency of divorce, separation, and remarriage

Within the last century (1875-1975), there has been a sixteenfold increase in the general divorce rate.[4] The U.S. divorce rate is now the highest for any country reporting to the United Nations.[5]

Since the mid-fifties, the divorce rate has increased by two-thirds and the remarriage rate by one-third, whereas the rate of first marriages has declined by one-tenth during this same period.[6]

Between 1920 and 1975 the proportion of all women in the population who were divorced increased sixfold. Even in the short period from 1970 to 1975, the proportion of previously married women ages twenty-five through fifty-four who were divorced increased 46 percent.[7]

The number of children under eighteen involved in divorce nearly tripled between 1953 and 1971. By the end of this period the number was close to a million.[8]

In the five years between 1970 and 1975 there was a 45 percent increase in the proportion of children under eighteen who were living with their mothers only.

In 1975 one out of every five children was living either with one parent only or without either parent.[9] According to the demographers Glick and Norton,

"Between one in four and one in three women around 30 years old today [1971] are likely to experience divorce during their lifetime. Moreover, five to ten percent of the thirty-year-old women are likely to obtain a second divorce."[10]

B. Statistics suggesting increasing postponement or avoidance of legal marriage, reduction of childbearing, or childbearing out of wedlock

In 1975 the number of births per 1,000 population was only 76 percent as high as ten years earlier (1965) and only 49 percent as high as the rate in 1910.[11]

According to 1973 birth rates, women can be expected to have an average of only 1.9 children by the time they complete their childbearing years. This figure is half the figure for 1957.[12]

With improved knowledge of birth control procedures, family size can be expected to decline even further as births are increasingly limited to wanted births. (According to a 1970 census survey, 13 percent of all white births and 27 percent of all black births to married women under 45 in the prior five years were unwanted births.[13])

The average household has shrunk in size from five persons in 1910 to less than three persons in 1975.[14]

Women are increasingly delaying marriage. The proportion of young women ages twenty to twenty-four who were still single increased by 42 percent between 1960 and 1975.[15]

Living in family units is declining.

According to the U.S. Bureau of the Census, "During the 15 years spanning 1960 to 1975, the number of one-person households had approximately doubled, from 6.9 million to 13.9 million." One-fifth of all households in 1975 consisted of persons living alone.[16]

According to Paul Glick, "A spectacular 8-fold increase occurred during the 1960's in the number of household heads who were reported as living apart from relatives while sharing their living quarters with an unrelated adult 'partner' (roommate or friend) of the opposite sex."[17]

The proportion of births that occurred outside of marriage more than tripled between 1950 and 1974.[18]

In 1971 the proportion of first births occurring outside of marriage was about double that in the late 1950s.[19]

"Three-quarters of all first pregnancies to teenagers were conceived premaritally," according to a 1971 national survey. "Almost three out of four of the women did not intend their conceptions." However, only 13 percent of this group "used contraception to avert it."[20]

Women are increasingly electing to interrupt their pregnancies. Before the liberalization of abortion laws, legal abortions averaged approximately 2 per 1,000 births.[21] By 1973 there were 239 legal abortions for each 1,000 live births. In the short period between 1970 and 1974 there was almost a five-fold increase in the number of legal abortions reported.[22]

C. Other suggestive statistics

The proportion of married women who were working or seeking work even though they had both a husband present in the home and children under six increased more than threefold between 1950 and 1975.[23]

According to the Harris poll, "The percentage of women who believe that 'taking care of a home and raising children is more rewarding for women than having a job' has declined from 71 to 51% in the past five years."[24]

Women are increasingly trying to escape from their marriages. Ed. Goldfader of the Tracers Company of America reports that "ten years ago we were looking for 300 runaway husbands for every wife who fled. By 1973 the number of women caught up to the number of men, and last year we were searching for 147 more missing wives than husbands."[25]

More executives are refusing to relocate. Important among the objections cited, according to *The New York Times*, are the adverse effects of uprooting on the family. One organization that moves families reported that "in 1973 37 percent of 300 customer companies ran into some refusal by employees to relocate. In 1974 the figure jumped to 57 percent. In 1972, there had not been enough of a problem to take a poll on it."[26]

"A veritable revolution" has occurred in the use of contraception by married couples, according to Dr. Charles F. Westoff, director of the Office of Population Research at Princeton. For this group, he says, "We are rapidly approaching universal, highly effective contraceptive practice." A recent survey that he codirected showed that "in 1973, 70 percent of couples were using some method of contraception" and that "sterilization . . . [is] the . . . fastest-growing contraceptive technique among married Americans. . . . Among couples in which the wife is 30 years old or older sterilization had become the chief method by 1973."[27]

Based on extended personal interviews with 437 "significant" Americans, Cuber and Harroff conclude that "by the middle years, there is a pervasive and candid recognition among many--perhaps a third--that their mate choices had not been wise."[28]

According to Herbert Otto, "Some marriage specialists estimate that anywhere from 40 to 60 percent of all marriages are at any given time 'subclinical.' The couples involved could materially benefit from the help of a marriage counselor, but they never reach a clinic."[29]

IV. THE SOURCES OF FAMILY CHANGE

A. Technological changes

Advances in techniques for birth control now make control of conception feasible. The population explosion makes such control necessary. (57; 89, pp. 301-305; 119)

Abortion is becoming more easily available.

Research on sex has helped to dispel

myths and to collapse taboos in this area. (15, 57, 58, 69, 88, 100, 109)

The increasing life-span accentuates the problem of monotony in marriage.

Family functions are being lost to industry, thus decreasing a man's need for a spouse. Housekeeping chores are also being reduced with technical aids.

Urban crowding makes for smaller living units that often preclude inclusion of three generations in one household.

The dependence on the family unit for economic security has lessened.

The need of industry for high family mobility leads to the breaking of ties with the extended family, creates a conflict of interest between spouses over moving, and increases the demands on the family as the major source of intensive, intimate relationships.

Increases in living standards and prosperity give people more freedom of choice and a wider range of choices.

Expansion of higher education for women also increases the options open to women.

Increasingly, sexually stimulating material is being commercially exploited.

The employment of women outside the home greatly increases the number and variety of men-women contacts.

The rapid tempo of change leads to fear of permanency.

An increasing variety of occupations is being opened to women, thus increasing the attraction of career alternatives to marriage.

B. Women's Liberation Movement (1, 7, 8, 15, 27, 30, 33, 36, 39, 44, 73, 110, 125)

Challenge to "mystique of motherhood" (120, 121)
Challenge to traditional sex roles; demand of women that men share fully the household and child-rearing functions and demand that they be free from exploitation both in and outside the home
Demand for equal job access and equal remuneration
Insistence on freedom to choose a life-style other than marriage and children without being termed a failure (1, 7, 8, 26, 27, 113)
Push for freedom from dependence on men
Challenge to many hidden and subtle aspects of sex discrimination

C. Widespread disaffection with monogamous family pattern

Decrease in sense of commitment or complete lack of commitment; movement toward insecure, unstable, open-ended relationships
Stress on individual growth and development and depth in relationships, with downgrading of marriage as growth-limiting (20, 35, 87, 88)
Unwillingness to accept boredom and devitalization in marriage
Experimentation with fluid, idealistic searching and attempts to annihilate interpersonal distance
Insistence of many that they have a choice of family patterns (among pluralistic alternatives)
Widespread group efforts to revitalize

monogamous relationships (see section II)

V. ALTERNATE FORMS FOR FAMILY LIVING

A. Extended heterosexual cohabitation (2, 6, 10, 45, 63, 68, 72, 110, 117)

1. Extent and trends

Cohabitation is both more common and more open than formerly.

In a recent poll 27 percent of those interviewed approved of living together out of wedlock; 15 percent reported that it was at least somewhat likely that they themselves would do it.[30]

Colleges tacitly encourage cohabitation by providing mixed-sex dormitories and by being increasingly permissive about off-campus living.

Macklin reports that 34 percent of a sample of underclassmen indicated having experienced cohabitation. (72, p. 464)

Ald estimates that as many as 42 percent of students on the campuses he visited were cohabiting or had cohabited or were receptive to such a relationship. (2, p. 13)

Henz and Hudson reported, also for a student sample, that 29 percent of the men and 18 percent of the women were currently cohabiting or had cohabited. (45, p. 722)

2. Types

Sharing room or apartment but not bed

Sharing room and bed
Sharing both room and bed with several others

3. <u>Philosophy as to benefits</u>

Provides opportunity for testing personal and sexual compatibility
Facilitates search for meaningful relationship with opposite sex
Promotes self-understanding and maturity
Encourages openness, nonsecrecy
Permits avoidance of commitment to marriage by those who do not see a permanent arrangement as a viable alternative for them at a given time
Preferred to weekend "shacking up," promiscuity, or superficiality of formal dating; therefore, appeals to serious, intense people

4. <u>Problems experienced</u>

Finding compatible mate
Dealing with parental disapproval (or concealment from parents by elaborate arrangements)
Lack of privacy, inadequate space, poor living arrangements, disagreements with partner, friction with other apartment mates
Feelings of lack of belonging, insecurity about the future
Feelings of guilt
Feelings of being trapped or used
Frequent abortions, unwanted pregnancies, and a variety of sexual problems

Delay in identity development because of overinvolvement in relationship
Jealousy (of mate's other activities)
Temporary character of many liaisons, with trauma at point of termination

5. Evaluation by participants

More than half of the group studied by Macklin consider their relationships of this type to have been "very successful." Only one-fourth would not want to repeat the experience with the same person. (72, p. 469)
All indicated that "they would not consider marriage without having experienced living with the person first." (72, pp. 469-70)

B. Single parenthood by choice (male or female) (51, 59, 106)

1. Types

Deliberate conception (Single parent purposefully conceives, bears, and rears child out of wedlock.)
Unintentional conception (Single parent conceives child unintentionally but chooses to bear and rear child as a single parent.)
Conception by a third party (Single parent adopts child borne by another.) (51, 106)

(Traditional types of single parenthood based on accidental death, separation, or divorce of spouse or on unwanted out-of-wedlock pregnancy with no decision to keep child are not covered in this review of alternate life-styles.)

2. Philosophy as to benefits

Separates role of wife and mother, thus making parenthood available independently of choice of marriage; option needed to support the right of each person to choose his own life-style

Liberates women from limitations to personal freedom and growth often imposed by marriage without denying them the opportunity to experience parenting; fosters their independent identity

Permits a person with outstanding aptitude for child rearing who is precluded for some reason from marrying to contribute as a parent

Helps men who choose this option to escape the limitations of a stereotyped male role

Encourages extended family relationships, a communal style of living, and openness in child care arrangements

Fosters a risk-taking, experiential style of living

3. Extent

Extent unknown, but related data suggest frequent choice of this option:

"Well over half of the single, pregnant women who contact social agencies decide to keep their babies rather than give them up for adoption." (59, p. 9)

In a recent poll, 7 percent of the respondents reported that they would be at least "somewhat likely" to have a child out of wedlock.[31]

In 1973, 13 out of every 100 births occurred out of wedlock.[32]

Adoption by single applicants is rare. (106, p. 105)

4. Problems

Lack of a partner with whom to share day-to-day child care, child-rearing problems, major decision making, and coping with crises

Likelihood of reduced income (single parent must be both parent and breadwinner)

Probability of parental disapproval, with consequent loss of parental support

Loneliness, isolation, and confinement; inherent limitations on social life

Absence of adequate child-care supports (for example, day care, homemaker service)

Conflict of child-care responsibilities with social needs of single parent

Possible conflict between needs of parent that led to choice of single parenthood and child's need for parental concern for his own needs

Increased difficulty in maintaining discipline and avoiding overdependence and overprotection of child

Difficulty of providing child with adequate role models of the opposite sex and direct experience with

husband-wife interaction in a nuclear family
Sense of deprivation that the child may experience over missing one parent

C. Voluntary childlessness (8, 13, 39, 78, 107, 120, 121)

1. Philosophy as to benefits

Provides a liberating alternative to parenthood, thereby increasing the options open to women and improving their self-image
Increases flexibility, freedom, and mobility of wife for pursuit of career; avoids career discontinuity; improves wife's chances of career success
Eliminates the financial, emotional, physical, and time demands of child rearing and its inherent risks; avoids the intrusion of these demands on husband-wife intimacies
Avoids negative psychological consequences of involuntary motherhood for both mothers and children
Makes it socially acceptable for persons to avoid parenthood when, for biological, psychological, financial, or other reasons, they would make poor parents
Provides a method of population control that is consistent with individual freedom and personal choice

2. Extent and trends

Poll results:
"Three in four Americans believe 'it is perfectly all right to be mar-

ried and to choose not to have children.'"[33]

One parent in ten reports that "if they had it to do over again, they would not have children."[34]

One woman in twenty thinks that marriage without children "would offer the most satisfying and interesting life."[35] One in twenty-five ages eighteen through twenty-four intends to remain childless.[36]

Census findings:

More than one woman in eight who is or has been married at some time ends her childbearing years childless.[37]

The proportion of families with no children under eighteen increased by 7 percent in the fifteen-year period between 1960 and 1975.[38]

Promotion of childlessness as a desirable option has become a new area of advocacy (stand of the National Organization of Non-Parents--NON).

3. <u>Factors contributing to trends</u>

Difficulty of combining child rearing and significant career achievement

High costs of child rearing (78, 120)

Change in attitudes about importance of having children

Increasing recognition, based on research findings, that child-rearing stages of the family life cycle are associated with reduced happiness (7, 8, 13)

4. Problems

Coping with strong social pressures toward parenthood (including the "motherhood mystique") (120)
Facing the negative public image of the childless state and pressures to explain choice (120)
Loss of growth-stimulating experiences of parenthood
Loss of help of children in emergencies and in old age
Possibility of later regret of the decision to remain childless after childbearing years are past
Enormous social consequences if voluntary childlessness should become a widespread pattern

D. Hippie life-style (other than communes) (10, pp. 74-78; 29, pp. 90-91; 33)

1. Philosophy

Antiestablishment; rejecting society's values and sexual restraints
Dropping out of productive process
Glorification of poverty
Minimizing differences between sexes, for example, in dress and roles
Sharing ("free stores," shared "pads," food, group sex)
Nonviolence (idealistic "flower children")
Mind expansion through drugs; psychedelic culture
Emancipation from parental directives

2. Problems

Detachment from parents and extended family and break in intergenerational communication

Heavy drug use--"acid cult," "speed freaks," "bad scenes"
Exploitation by noncontributing members, pimps, and phonies ("plastic hippies")
Tendency of hippie areas to be taken over by criminal element
Isolation from long-term community ties and community acceptance

E. Communes--intentional communities (29, 47, 50, 52, 56, 62, 65, 66, 76, 86, 93, 94, 108, 109, 111, 112, 115, 117, 118, 119, 122)

1. Philosophy

Idealization of community, togetherness, equality
Glorification of simple living, sharing, pooling of property, common tasks
Back to nature: vegetarianism, organic farming, natural childbirth
Rejection of technology and social conventions (for example, avoidance of full-time jobs, use of television)
Utopian flavor (similar to utopian communities in past centuries): idealism, nonviolence, mysticism, new life-styles, women's liberation
Heavy investment in interpersonal relations: "people come first"
Emphasis on group processes, self-revelation, intimacy, experiental approach
Innovative approaches to child rearing

2. Extent

Estimate: "Between 1965 and 1970 more than two thousand communes were established" [in the United States]. (47, p. xiii)

Participants: mostly people under forty

One respondent in seven, in the 1974 poll of the Institute of Life Insurance, approved of communal living. For those under twenty-five the proportion was three in ten.[39]

3. Types

Location: urban or rural (agricultural)

Age composition: young to aged, but usually limited in age range

Political orientation: Marxist, Maoist, anticapitalist, counterculture, nonpolitical

Religious orientation: convervative, liberal, Asian, or none

Amount of discipline: heavy to none; some anarchistic; some based on authority

Leadership: charismic, shared, hierarchical, or minimal

Sexual pattern: almost anything from monogamy to group sex, group marriage, or total sexual freedom

Use of drugs: drug oriented, not drug oriented, or oriented to limited drug use

Life-style: hippie to conservative

4. Problems

Seeing that basic living tasks get done, especially coverage of unpleasant tasks, clean-up, and maintenance of order

Balancing responsibility to group against meeting own needs

Assuring essential minimum of economic support in spite of withdrawal from economy

Conflict over food, money, task allocation, space, noise, and privacy

Accommodating to loss of members and internal conflict

Conflict with parents, extended family, neighbors, and community

Coping with building codes, fire codes, and sanitation violations

Relation to welfare structure; denial of food stamps and welfare benefits (because not considered families)

Denial of tax benefits available to traditional family units

Lack of legal supports (for property, family rights, distribution of communal property when commune disbands)

Age segregation

Difficulties in establishing paternity

Jealousy of parents over attention shown to own children by other commune members; sexual jealousy

Effect on children, especially of instability of group and consequent nomadic life, plus lack of material supports

Resolution of who takes the children when commune breaks up

Exploitation by drop-ins--those who come to take all they can, give little, and lack consideration for others in the group

Instability of communes in general

5. Duration
(52, 65, 108)

If based on anarchistic concepts of freedom, if each does his "own thing," with integrative philosophy and organization lacking, communes are short-lived, usually breaking up within a year.

If formed around a growth-and-learning center, where focus is on group interaction, explicit values, and fixed daily routines, they tend to be more stable--at least for staff (although guest members may be transient).

"Failure is usually related to one of four issues: lack of leadership, lack of means of handling internal disputes, lack of ideology, or external repression." (65, p. 150)

"Those communes based on authority, particularly religious authority, often endure and survive even against vigorous opposition from the outside world." (108, p. 530)

In general, most commune dwellers, in spite of their many problems, "have no intention of going straight or reentering the dominant culture." (108, p. 530)

F. Group or multilateral marriages
(18, 19, 20, 41, 66, 86, 91, 93, 94, 109, 115, 117)

1. Definition and extent

A multilateral marriage is "a marriage of at least three individuals, each of whom [considers him-self/herself to be] married to at least two other members of the conjugal unit." (18, p. 159)

There are no statistics available about the extent of multilateral marriages, but they are relatively infrequent. Constantine estimates that early in 1972 there were about a thousand multilateral marriages. (19, p. 32)

2. Philosophy as to benefits

Promotes personality development and self-actualization through intimate interaction with more than one type of person

Provides sexual variety without sacrificing depth of relationship and continuity or requiring secrecy

Promotes sexual and social equality between the sexes

Provides for broader role sharing, a broader economic base, and security of multiple love relationships

Provides children with multiple (hence less rigid) role models and multiple emotional resources while lessening child-rearing responsibility of any one parent

3. Characteristics
(19, pp. 31, 67, 150, 249-51)

Model pattern: four adults (two pairs); range is from three to six adults plus children

Children: more than four out of five groups include children, typically two or three

Ages of adult participants: twenty-one to fifty-nine; median, for males, thirty-one years; for females, twenty-eight years

Duration of groups: 44 percent still together after one year; maximum reported duration of extant groups, five years; no traceable attempts at multilateral marriages prior to 1966

4. Problems

Finding suitable mates

Difficulties in decision making because of mixed interests, number of different persons involved, and traditions of autonomy

Scheduling of sex: fixed rotation, free choice, rotation of choice, group sex, or some combination

Finding large enough housing units

Maintaining a united front by multiple parental figures, deciding on issues of discipline

For children, dealing with a more complex family identiciation process

Time invested in meeting group needs and in decision making

Conflicting interests involved in major decisions

Jealousy (about time and possessions of others)

Lack of legal base (a long-term problem)

In general, the high levels of complexity and intensity involved in maintaining satisfying intimate relations among so many people

G. Swinging (organized mate swapping) (5, 17, 27, 28, 37, 60, 66, 109, 115)

1. <u>Philosophy as to benefits</u>

Provides sexual variety within marriage without cheating or guilt
Protects anonymity with respect to outside world

2. <u>Extent</u>

Regular swingers are estimated at one-half to one percent of the total population. (5, p. 20)
Occasional swingers are estimated by some researchers at as many as eight million. (5, p. 19)
Of 2,000 persons who participated in a 1972 survey, only 2 percent of the married males and less than 2 percent of the married females had ever participated in mate swapping with their spouses.[40]
It is predicted that "even under optimal social conditions only some 15 to 25 percent of married couples would be attracted to it [swinging]." (5, p. 290)

3. <u>Participation</u>

Major group attracted: white, middle-class married couples, mostly under forty, who are otherwise "straight" but alienated
Duration: participation usually temporary, two to five years
Participants: usually not idealistic and not related to drug culture
Focus: recreation with hedonistic emphasis

4. <u>Types</u>

Size of group: ranges from occasional exchanges between two couples to exchanges involving large impersonal groups
Location: city or suburban; may also include campus and commune
Sexual relations: open (within group) or closed (in privacy)

5. <u>How organized</u>

Privately--through advertising in swinging magazines or through swinging bars or clubs
Special language developed for advertising to assure type of sexual practices preferred
Screening--by telephone, through an initial formal meeting without sex, by recommendations from previous contacts, and by personal acquaintance
Protection of marriages by keeping swinging contacts limited to a very few meetings with any given couple

6. <u>Values (as reported by participants)</u> (5, pp. 279-83)

Improved social and sexual relationships (reported by majority)
Increased sexual excitement through continual replay of mating game
Mutual sharing between spouses of interests and projects in this area
Reduction of sexual inhibitions, help in working through voyeurism
Provision of sexual variety in a manner compatible with continuation

of marriages (swinging usually not destructive of a marriage)

7. Problems

Tendency of swingers to be too mechanistic and uninvolved in their sexual relations--"trophy hunters"
Lack of intimacy in relationships fostered by need to change partners continually
Tolerance required for wide range of sexual techniques and for nude exposure in groups
Time required by the necessity to keep making new arrangements
Competitive position in which man is placed: difficulty in living up to self-ideal and masculine fantasies and in responding sexually with timing and frequency required for group parties
Jealousy, guilt, and threat to marriage (28)
Bartering of women (use of wife as a trade-off for sexual varietism for man)
Hazard of discovery (wish of most couples to keep children from learning that they are swinging, fear that police will answer advertisements, fear of consequences to professional position if discovered)
Risk of traumatic experiences
Spreading of venereal disease
Need to stop when children are wanted (to assure that father can be identified)
Disagreements between partners about participation in swinging

H. Homosexual pairing
(25, 27, 33, 42, 44, 46, 57, 58, 59, 69, 82, 117, 119, 124)

1. Trends

More open acceptance and more self-acceptance of homosexuality
Earlier "coming out" in "gay" world, less policy of silence, more militancy
Some dropping of "butch" and "chick" role differentiations
Beginning use of formal church ceremonies to provide religious sanction for homosexual "unions"
Pressure for acceptance of adoption of children by homosexual couples (59)
Pressures for legal changes to permit any form of sexual relationship between consenting adults
Pressures for elimination of housing, job, and other discrimination

2. Extent

No reliable current figures.
Kinsey in 1948 estimated that 4 percent of white males in the population were "exclusively homosexual . . . throughout their lives after the onset of adolescence" and that 10 percent were "more or less exclusively homosexual . . . for at least three years between the ages of 16 and 55."[41]
Hunt concludes from his 1972 survey that there has been no significant increase in homosexuality since the Kinsey study. (49, pp. 303-17)

3. Problems

Social segregation and stigmatization
Housing discrimination
Job discrimination
Legal handicaps and exclusion from tax and welfare benefits applicable to families
Lack of sufficient services for help in interpersonal problems
Strained relation to churches (69)
Impaired self-image

I. Other emerging patterns for extramarital sexual intimacy

Changing attitudes toward infidelity and toward extramarital and comarital sex (48, 49, 80, 109; see also I-B-10)
The cocktail-lounge model for semiserious extramarital relationships (10, pp. 68-71)
The new "swinging" singles (10, pp. 66-68; see also V-G)
Increased discussion of polygamy and polyandry as possible alternatives (18, 19, 41, 53, 57, 80, 86, 93, 98, 99, 119)
Increased acceptance of intimate friendships and intimate networks with sexual sharing (94, 95, 109, 118)

VI. IMPLICATIONS FOR SERVICE, RESEARCH, AND POLICY

A. Extent of contact of family service agencies with those involved in the new life-styles

Contact is minimal because these groups tend to shy away from family agencies out of fear that agencies will pressure them into the traditional mold or define them as "sick."

Most problems related to these experiments come to agencies indirectly through applications from concerned parents and through contact with those in enough trouble to be ready to consider returning to more traditional ways.

B. Needs of these groups

Those involved in these new types of family living encounter many of the same types of relationship, sexual, and reality problems that make trouble for more traditional families.

They need sympathetic counseling on a wide range of problems (without fear of being rejected, pressured, or being labeled "sick").

Many sad experiences are alleged to have occurred when counseling help was sought.

Their parents need help in understanding their children's behavior and attitudes and in coping with new types of intergenerational relationships.

Their children need parental understanding and acceptance.

Those involved in these experiments also need help in coping with an antagonistic culture, plus advocacy help in the larger society on behalf of their special needs.

They also need help in evaluating their living-together experiences. (6)

C. Changes required in practice and other services (16, 20, 28, 30, 32, 38, 43, 60, 69, 70, 71, 76, 79, 83, 84, 85, 87, 90, 96, 102, 105, 116)

Sufficient openness in attitudes and values, plus sufficient informed knowledge and interest, on the part of staff to permit the extension of services to those involved in the experiments in ways they can accept (69); new initiatives in staff development to foster these changes (43)

A revised theoretical base for treatment to accommodate to new types of problems, new underlying dynamics, new sources of stress, and new attitudes toward sexual deviance

Increased skills in the new group approaches because of great interest of young people in encounter groups, sensitivity groups, T-groups, marathons, marriage enrichment groups, growth groups, and so forth

Increased competence in articulating and promoting positives in marital relationships, such as better communication, positive reinforcement and growth, revised living patterns, and marriage enrichment generally, plus family life education for marriage and child rearing whether in new or old types of settings (32, 38, 84, 103)

Increased competence in counseling in the sexual area in the context of the greatly increased diversity in sexual practices

Increased knowledge about how to cope with new problems (for example, intergenerational conflict over new life-styles, drugs, the complexities of interaction in multilateral families, communes)

Increased attention to and skill in birth control and abortion counseling

Development of new methods of outreach and service delivery to provide nontraditional families with the benefits of counseling

D. Research needs
(6, 16, 83)

Knowledge about such aspects of communal and other group-living arrangements as the day-to-day interaction problems, values, service needs, and parent-child relationships

Longitudinal studies to ascertain the strengths and deficits of specific life-styles--their permanency, effect on children, consequences for self-identity, and so on (The research problem here is to cope with the rapidity with which these groups form and disappear.)

Studies of how to improve the choice of marital partners and decisions about termination of marriage

Studies to find new and more acceptable techniques for fertility control regardless of family life-style

E. Shifts needed in institutional arrangements and social policy
(8, 16, 38, 74, 83, 84, 116, 117, 118)

Supports for new roles for both men and women, for example, larger housing units adapted to larger family units and convenient to location of work, plus a variety of group services, such as expanded child-care services; also training of group child-care personnel and part-time jobs for both men and women

Improved legal, economic, and social supports and protections for these new family forms--for example, legalization of new forms; establishment of property rights, inheritance rights, welfare rights, social security rights, and child rights; plus social and religious supports

Legal and economic supports for those assuming care-taking functions beyond the nuclear family unit

Portable insurance for adults and their children (to accommodate to sequential marriages)

Expanded opportunities for both men and women for the types of education that will prepare both sexes to combine vocational roles with marriage, homemaking, and child-rearing functions

Policies that promote equal opportunity for both sexes on all fronts, including policy making, and discouraging of sex-role stereotyping

Policies in industry and business that accommodate to families with dual careers and support the welfare of families generally

Encouragement of simplification of home maintenance tasks and deemphasis of material possessions

Extensive public supports for responsible family planning

Modernization of marriage and divorce laws

Elimination of mandatory retirement age

Working out of value positions related to these new family forms

F. What agencies have to give that is potentially valuable in relation to these many challenges

The basic fundamentals of what makes for good human relationships in an intimate interpersonal interaction apply regardless of the structural pattern or legal status of the group involved.

These principles have long been known to family counselors and are now part of their basic "practice wisdom." (An analysis of the characteristics of a good marriage identified such essentials as good communication, reciprocity in need satisfaction, constructive handling and resolving of conflicts, effective decision making, competence in coping with stress, and flexibility in meeting change.[42]

Family counselors have well-developed skills in facilitating needed changes in these areas in a wide variety of problem situations.

With relatively minor adaptations, these skills can be extended to serve much more adequately than at present the special needs of those who are pioneering new forms of family living and sexual intimacy.

NOTES

1. William J. Lederer and Don D. Jackson, *The Mirages of Marriage* (New York: W. W. Norton & Co., 1968), p. 13.

2. Mervyn Cadwallader, "Marriage as a Wretched Institution," *Atlantic Monthly*, November 1966, pp. 62-66.

3. Harold T. Christensen and Christina F. Gregg, "Changing Sex Norms in America and Scandinavia," *Journal of Marriage and Family Living* 32 (November 1970): 616-27; and Kenneth L. Cannon and Richard Long, "Premarital Sexual Behavior in the Sixties," *Journal of Marriage and Family Living* 33 (February 1971): 36-49.

4. Computed from the *Monthly Vital Statistics Report* 24, no. 12 (4 March 1976): 1; and Paul H. Jacobson, *American Marriage and Divorce* (New York: Rinehart & Co., 1959), p. 90. The provisional figure for 1975 was 4.8 divorces per 1,000 population; for the limited area for which divorce figures were available in 1875, the corresponding figure was 0.3.

5. United Nations, *Demographic Yearbook, 1973* (New York: United Nations, 1974), pp. 371-72.

6. Paul C. Glick and Arthur J. Norton, "Perspectives on the Recent Upturn in Divorce and Remarriage," *Demography* 10 (August 1973): 301-14. Trends cited reflect the number of divorces per thousand married women under forty-five years of age, the number of remarriages per thousand divorced or widowed women under fifty-five years of age, and the number of first marriages per thousand single women under forty-five years of age.

7. Computed from U.S., Bureau of the Census, *Statistical Abstract of the United States: 1975*, 96th ed. (Washington, D.C.: Government Printing Office, 1975), p. 38; and U.S., Bureau of the Census, *Current Population Reports*, ser. P-20, no. 287, "Marital Status and Living Arrangements: March 1975" (Washington, D.C.: Government Printing Office, 1975), pp. 5, 8.

8. Computed from Abbott L. Ferriss, *Indicators of Change in the American Family* (New York: Russell Sage Foundation, 1970), p. 123; and Paul C. Glick, *Some Recent Changes in American Families, Current Population Reports,* Special Studies, ser. P-23, no. 52 (Washington, D.C.: Government Printing Office, n.d.), p. 10.

9. Computed from *Current Population Reports,* ser. P-20, no. 287, p. 6.

10. Glick and Norton, "Perspectives on the Recent Upturn," p. 311.

11. Computed from *Statistical Abstract: 1975,* p. 51; and *Monthly Vital Statistics Report* 24, no. 12 (4 March 1976): 1. (Figures for 1975 are provisional.)

12. Glick, *Some Recent Changes,* p. 2.

13. *Statistical Abstract: 1975,* p. 57. Data were originally compiled by the U.S. Commission on Population Growth and the American Future.

14. Figure for 1910 is from Glick, *Some Recent Changes,* p. 13; figure for 1975 is from U.S., Bureau of the Census, *Current Population Reports,* ser. P-20, no. 291, "Household and Family Characteristics: March 1975" (Washington, D.C.: Government Printing Office, 1976), p. 1.

15. Computed from *Current Population Reports*, ser. P-20, no. 287, p. 2.

16. *Current Population Reports*, ser. P-20, no. 291, p. 2.

17. Computed from Glick, *Some Recent Changes*, p. 13; and *Monthly Vital Statistics Report* 24, no. 11, supp. 2 (13 February 1976): 10, 11.

18. Computed from *Statistical Abstract: 1975*, p. 57.

19. Glick, *Some Recent Changes*, p. 3.

20. Melvin Zelnik and John F. Kauter, "The Resolution of Teenage First Pregnancies," *Family Planning Perspectives* 6 (Spring 1974): 74-80. Quotations are from pages 75 and 77.

21. Estimate by Christopher Tietze cited in Edward A. Duffy, *The Effect of Changes in the State Abortion Laws* (Washington, D.C.: U.S. Department of Health, Education, and Welfare, 1971), p. 4.

22. Christopher Tietze et al., *Provisional Estimates of Abortion Need and Services in the Year Following the 1973 Supreme Court Decisions: United States, Each State and Metropolitan Area* (New York: Alan Guttmacher Institute, Planned Parenthood Federation of America, 1975), pp. 7-8.

23. Computed from *Statistical Abstract: 1975*, p. 347.

24. Harris Survey Release, "Changing Views on the Role of Women," dated 11 December 1975.

25. Margie Casady, "Runaway Wives: Husbands Don't Pick Up the Danger Signals Their Wives Send Out," *Psychology Today*, May 1975, p. 42.

26. "More Executives Refusing to Relocate," *New York Times*, 7 November 1975, pp. 1, 15.

27. "Study Finds Sterilization Gains Fastest of Birth-Curb Methods," *New York Times*, 5 May 1976, p. 22. Statements based on national fertility studies conducted by Charles F. Westoff and Norman B. Ryder for the National Center for Health Statistics.

28. John F. Cuber and Peggy B. Harroff, *The Significant Americans: A Study of Sexual Behavior Among the Affluent* (New York: Appleton-Century-Crofts, 1965), p. 88.

29. Herbert A. Otto, "Has Monogamy Failed?" *Saturday Review*, 25 April 1970, p. 23.

30. Research Services Institute of Life Insurance, *Public Attitudes Toward the Family, Having Children, New Life Styles, Social Movements, Control over Important Areas of Life: Selected Findings from National Surveys, Spring 1974* (New York: Institute of Life Insurance, 1974), p. 7.

31. Ibid.

32. *Statistical Abstract: 1975*, p. 57. Figure is provisional.

33. *Current Social Issues--The Public's View: Findings from a Series of National Surveys, Spring 1975* (New York: Institute of Life Insurance, 1976), p. 7.

34. Mary McLaughlin, "Parents Who Wouldn't Do It Again" (Report of a Gallup Poll, in "Right Now" column), *McCall's*, November 1975, pp. 17, 38.

35. Roper Organization, *The Virginia Slims American Women's Opinion Poll*, vol. 3, *A Survey of the Attitudes of Women on Marriage, Di-*

vorce, the Family and America's Changing Sexual Morality (New York: Roper Organization, 1974), p. 33.

36. *Statistical Abstract: 1975*, p. 56.

37. Ibid., p. 54. Statement based on fact that 13 percent of ever-married women ages fifty through fifty-nine are childless.

38. Computed from U.S., Bureau of the Census, *Current Population Reports*, ser. P-20, no. 291, "Household and Family Characteristics: March 1975" (Washington, D.C.: Government Printing Office, 1976), p. 4.

39. *Current Social Issues*, p. 20.

40. Morton Hunt, *Sexual Behavior in the 1970's* (New York: Dell Publishing Co., 1975, paperback ed.), p. 37.

41. Alfred C. Kinsey, Wardell B. Pomeroy, and Clyde E. Martin, *Sexual Behavior in the Human Male* (Philadelphia: W. B. Saunders Co., 1948), p. 651.

42. Sheila Day, "Profile Models Contrasting the Characteristics of Ideally 'Healthy' and Extremely 'Unhealthy' Marriages, as Seen by Caseworkers," an analysis prepared for the FSAA Project on the Treatment of Marital Problems, mimeographed (New York: Family Service Association of America, 1964).

ANNOTATED BIBLIOGRAPHY

BY

EMILY BRADSHAW

The intent of this bibliography is to direct its users to appropriate references on specific topics of interest relating to the subject of "Marriage and the Family Under Challenge." This bibliography should not be considered comprehensive, nor should its references be considered especially recommended readings.

Emphasis has been given to literature appearing in the scholarly journals rather than to book material.

Annotations are intended primarily to convey the authors' viewpoints, perspectives, and, in many instances, proposals for alternate forms for family living. Unless otherwise indicated, all quotations are those of the authors.

1. Adams, Margaret. "The Single Woman in Today's Society: A Reappraisal." *American Journal of Orthopsychiatry* 41 (October 1971): 776-86.

"The single woman is defined, and her role in society--particularly within the larger context of the 'normal' woman's role--is delineated in terms of the social and psychological problems encountered by members of this minority group. The benefits of being a single woman in today's society, and their value as a model for the women's liberation movement, are discussed. It is concluded that current trends are moving in the direction of obviating differences in status and self-concept between single and married women."

2. Ald, Roy. *Sex Off Campus*. New York: Grosset & Dunlap, 1969.

Twelve unmarried student couples, each of whom was sharing living quarters, "tell their own stories--how they feel about their parents, their new sexual freedom, and the broad sociological impact of their actions." (Publisher) This book began in the form of an article for a popular national magazine.

3. Alpenfels, Ethel J. "Progressive Monogamy: An Alternate Pattern?" In *The Family in Search of a Future: Alternate Models for Moderns*, edited by Herbert A. Otto, pp. 67-73. New York: Appleton-Century-Crofts, 1970.

The author "contends that hidden cultural values motivate human behavior and considers progressive monogamy (the practice of taking several partners, one at a time) as an alternate structure for the familial system." (Editor)

4. Athanasion, Robert; Phillip Shaver; and Carol Tavris. "Sex." *Psychology Today*, July 1970, pp. 39-52.

Report on more than 20,000 responses to a questionnaire about sexual attitudes and practices.

5. Bartell, Gilbert. *Group Sex: A Scientist's Eyewitness Report on the American Way of Swinging*. New York: Peter H. Wyden, 1971.

"This book deals with mate-swapping as seen through the eyes of an anthropologist" who "studied more than 280 housewives, salesmen, lawyers, teachers and other 'swingers' in the Midwest, Texas and Louisiana." (Publisher)

6. Berger, Miriam E. "Trial Marriage: Harnessing the Trend Constructively." *The Family Coordinator* 20 (January 1971): 38-43.

"The concept of trial marriage is traced historically and anthropologically. . . . To harness the trend constructively the author recommends that young people who have had a living-together experience evaluate it with a counselor in order to gain insight about their potentialities as mates. Research is recommended to determine whether trial marriage is a valid preparation for marriage."

7. Bernard, Jessie. *The Future of Marriage*. New York: World Publishing Co., 1972.

The author "gathers the facts about marriage as it has evolved and as it is lived in

America today." She believes that "'men and women will continue to want to celebrate their mutuality, will continue to want intimacy, will continue to want to experience that mystic unity. . . .' The marriage of the future will, however, be different, as different as the type of relationships it will encompass. It may no longer be a lifetime contract, demand sexual fidelity, or even involve the sharing of one household. . . . It will, certainly, if it is to survive, recognize the autonomy of women and their greater economic independence." (Publisher)

8. ———. *The Future of Motherhood*. New York: Dial Press, 1974.

In this book, the author writes "about the changing role of women in modern society. . . . She argues for more sharing of the mothering between husband and wife, for more and better day care centers, and feels that both children and society can profit by opening up 'motherhood' to men as well as women." (*Publishers Weekly*)

9. ———. "Notes on Changing Life Styles, 1970-1974." *Journal of Marriage and the Family* 37 (August 1975): 582-600.

"The concept of life style connotes an ideology and set of values that find expression in, among other things, varying combinations of living arrangements and marital status. A recent publication of the Census Bureau prepared by Arthur Norton and his staff provides data to help illuminate changing life styles of divorced men and women between 1970 and 1974 by age. Additional data are also provided by age for life styles in 1974. The present paper addresses itself to certain aspects of these phenomena."

10. ———. "Present Demographic Trends and Structural Outcomes in Family Life Today." In *Marriage and Family Counseling: Perspective and Prospect*, edited by James A. Peterson, pp. 44-109. New York: Association Press, 1968.

    The author provided "an empirical analysis of the changes in demographic variables and structural form of the family during the last quarter of a century. She uses census data and past sociological studies to compare emergent family forms with past structures. In doing this she locates a number of new type 'families' which she labels with such terms as swingers, hippies, cocktail lounge and Berkeley models. She also brings the reader up-to-date regarding the gradients in births, marriages, divorces, etc. Some of her findings, such as the decline in teen-age marriages, the emergence of many pseudo-marital relationships, and the increasing incidence of marriage, are analyzed in depth." (Editor)

11. Birdwhistell, Ray L. "The Idealized Model of the American Family." *Social Casework* 51 (April 1970): 195-98.

    The author believes that "the concept of the ideal American family sets goals that are unattainable and may lead to tragic results in parent-child relationships and societal institutions." (Editor)

12. Brogan, Catherine Lee. "Changing Perspectives on the Role of Women," *Smith College Studies in Social Work* 42 (February 1972): 155-73.

"The purpose of this paper is to present what may be described as the traditional view of female psychology and woman's role in society along with some alternative formulations. Essentially the traditional view emphasizes innate biological factors and the alternatives emphasize the influence of a patriarchal culture, the socialization process, and the importance of economics, law and politics in shaping the prescribed social role for women and ultimately the individual woman's attitude toward herself."

13. Campbell, Angus. "The American Way of Mating; Marriage Sí, Children Only Maybe." *Psychology Today*, May 1975, pp. 37 ff.

"The positive effect of marriage and the stress-producing impact of children on the quality of life in America are two striking results" from a survey of 2,164 adults.

14. Cavan, Ruth Shonle. "Speculations on Innovations to Conventional Marriage in Old Age." *The Gerontologist* 13 (Winter 1973): 409-11.

"It is the thesis of this paper that old people have personal needs very similar to those of the young and that some of the innovations now being tried out by young people [nonmarital cohabitation, homosexuality or lesbian companionships, group marriage, communes, and comarital contracts] may be equally applicable to the old."

15. Chilman, Catherine S. "Some Psychological Aspects of Female Sexuality." *The Family Coordinator* 23 (April 1974): 123-31.

"Research pertaining to some psychosocial aspects of female sexuality is reviewed and the implications discussed."

16. Cogswell, Betty E., and Marvin B. Sussman. "Changing Family and Marriage Forms: Complications for Human Service Systems." *The Family Coordinator* 21 (October 1972): 505-16.

"In this paper, the position is taken that most human service systems operate with a value orientation that idealizes the traditional nuclear family. As a result, families which vary from this norm have many unmet needs. Initiating the discussion with the unusual family forms and marriage styles represented in this special issue, the range of more conventional variants is considered. The analysis indicates some of the problems nontraditional families have with current societal policies, legislation, and service organizations. Given are suggested changes which might support and enhance nontraditional as well as traditional family life."

17. Cole, Charles L., and Graham B. Spanier. "Induction into Mate Swapping: A Review." *Family Process* 12 (September 1973): 279-90.

"The question of how and why people become involved in co-marital sexual mate-swapping is examined in the larger context of familial behavior. The literature on other areas of sexuality is tapped for possible explanations of the mate-swapper phenomenon."

18. Constantine, Larry L., and Joan M. Constantine. "Group and Multilateral Marriage: Definitional Notes, Glossary and Annotated Bibliography." *Family Process* 10 (June 1971): 157-76.

The authors "define the phenomenon under current study in the Multilateral Relations Study Project and differentiate it from certain other related but different sociological phenomena."

19. ———— . *Group Marriage: A Study of Contemporary Multilateral Marriage.* New York: Macmillan Publishing Co., 1973.

"Larry and Joan Constantine are widely known for their studies of group marriage--or as they prefer, multilateral marriages. Their findings are necessarily based on a small sampling, for there aren't too many multilateral marriages around, many undoubtedly are under cover. They did find more than 100 groups and they met and corresponded with more than 30. Eleven served as the core of their basic group.

"The Constantines combined several approaches--extensive interviewing, the use of pencil-paper measuring instruments, and sometimes observations made through personal friendship. They wanted to know the kind of person interested in group marriage and why, how marriages were established and what problems and satisfactions are involved." (*Journal of Marriage and the Family*)

20. ———— and Sheldon K. Edelman. "Counseling Implications of Comarital and Multilateral Relations." *The Family Coordinator* 21 (July 1972): 267-78.

"Counselors may expect an increasing number of marriages to include open intimate involvement with others either as an adjunct to the marriage or as an integral part of it. Some elements of these marital styles are extensions of the more conventional dyadic relationship but others appear to be relatively unique or to require a new focus. Key problem areas are noted and application to counseling situations is made."

21. Cooper, David. *The Death of the Family.* New York: Pantheon Books, 1970.

A British psychoanalyst writes "on the need to abolish the traditional family and to substitute new forms of human relations." As stated in his introduction, the author "made no attempt to simplify some of the ambiguities and paradoxes of this book, since it is for those who have ears and can hear, but above all for those who can hear and then listen and then act."

22. Cox, Frank D. *American Marriage: A Changing Scene?* Dubuque, Iowa: William C. Brown Co., 1972.

This book is composed of twenty-seven readings grouped under the following headings: "Tomorrow's Morality," "The Romantic Ideal--Love and Marriage in America," "The Romantic Ideal--Ethnic, Cultural, and Class Differences," and "The Family of the Future." Commentaries by the author tie together the readings.

23. Cuber, John F. "Alternate Models from the Perspective of Sociology." In *The Family in Search of a Future: Alternate Models for Moderns,* edited by Herbert A. Otto, pp. 11-23. New York: Appleton-Century-Crofts, 1970.

The author "examines the question, 'Why consider alternatives?' and, from his perspective as a sociologist, concludes that we should accept 'pairings of the socially and physically mature . . . at any time at the mutual consent of the partners.' He proposes a variety of domicile arrangements for the married pairs, including provisions for parents living separated both from each other and from their children, with the state assuming broader child-rearing responsibilities." (Editor)

24. ——— . "Sexual Life-Styles and Fulfillments." In *The New Sexuality*, edited by Herbert A. Otto, pp. 143-54. Palo Alto, Calif.: Science and Behavior Books, 1971.

"The author finds that human sexual behavior and fulfillments take place within the framework of three sexual life-styles. He has called them the *sexually expressive*, the *sexually non-expressive*, and the *sexually ambivalent* styles. The author concludes that 'lasting, deep sexual fulfillment is rare in present American society regardless of the particular life-style.'" (Editor)

25. Dank, Barry M. "Coming Out in the Gay World." *Psychiatry* 34 (May 1971): 180-97.

This paper is devoted to exploring the emergence of the male homosexual identity. "The analysis is based on data obtained from lengthy interviews with 55 self-admitted homosexuals, on observations of and conversations with hundreds of homosexuals, and the results of a one-page questionnaire distributed to 300 self-admitted homosexuals attending a meeting of a homophile organization."

26. Davids, Leo. "North American Marriage: 1990." *The Futurist* 5 (October 1971): 190-94.

The author predicts that "two decades from now, marriage will be very different from what it is today. . . . Romantic love will have largely disappeared; there will be several kinds of marriage to choose from, and prospective parents will have to obtain licenses and undergo intensive training." (Editor)

27. DeLora, Jack R., and Joann S. DeLora, eds. *Intimate Life Styles: Marriage and Its Alternatives*, 2nd ed. Pacific Palisades, Calif.: Goodyear Publishing Co., 1975.

"This book of readings offers the reader the opportunity to explore a multitude of life styles available in our society today. The authors not only examine traditional patterns, but also alternate life styles, including singlehood, swinging, homosexuality. . . . The authors have included recent articles from popular magazines, publications of the Women's Liberation movement, the underground press, literary journals, homosexual literature, publications of singles' organizations. . . . Many well-known experts in the field of family development have contributed to the text." (*The Family Coordinator*)

28. Denfeld, Duane. "Dropouts from Swinging." *The Family Coordinator* 23 (January 1974): 45-49.

"A report from marriage counselors who have worked with swinging dropouts, this paper delineates some of the problems encountered."

29. Downing, Joseph. "The Tribal Family and the Society of Awakening." In *The Family in Search of a Future: Alternate Models for Moderns*, edited by Herbert A. Otto, pp. 119-35. New York: Appleton-Century-Crofts, 1970.

The author finds that "a different, although not necessarily new, family form is developing spontaneously through direct life experience." This form is the tribal family, a feature of a "diffusely evolving subculture [the author calls] the 'Society of Awakening.'" Tribal family members, according to the author, "try to reconstitute the loving, accepting, undemanding family unit which either was lost or never existed at all." The type of tribal family of "most current interest and notoriety is the so-called 'Hippie' group." Downing devotes much of his article to a description of the values and characteristics of this type of tribal family.

30. Duhl, Frederick J. "Changing Sex Roles--Concepts, Values, and Tasks." *Social Casework* 57 (February 1976): 87-92.

"It is suggested that family therapists question whether their energies should not be addressed to the arena of education and prevention rather than therapy." (Editor)

31. Eiduson, Bernice T.; Jerome Cohen; and Jannette Alexander. "Alternatives in Child Rearing in the 1970s." *American Journal of Orthopsychiatry* 43 (October 1973): 720-31.

"Drawing upon pilot interviews and home observations representing 50 families from rural and urban communes, single middle-class mothers, and 'unmarried marrieds,' the child-rearing practices, values and beliefs of counter-culture groups are examined and compared with those of two-parent nuclear families of the 1970s. Attitudes and practices of 'new' families bring into focus a number of fundamental issues, such as effects of multiple caretaking, anti-sexist attitudes, heightened interest in social relationships, and generalized trust of adults on the psychological growth of the child."

32. Farson, Richard E., et al. *The Future of the Family*. New York: Family Service Association of America, 1969.

Contents : "Physical Science Predicts and Projects," by Anthony J. Wiener; "Social Science Predicts and Projects," by Philip M. Hauser; "Philosophy Predicts and Projects," by Herbert Stroup; "Behavioral Science Predicts and Projects," by Richard E. Farson; "Symposium."

33. Feldman, Saul D., and Gerald W. Thielbar, eds. *Life Styles: Diversity in American Society*. Boston: Little, Brown and Co., 1972.

"This book--about beauty queens, rich people, homosexuals, tramps, Indians, Southern Californians, and other assorted Americans--examines the great diversity of life styles within American society." (Editors)

34. Fleischmann, Karl. "Marriage by Contract: Defining the Terms of Relationship." *Family Law Quarterly* 8 (Spring 1974): 27-49.

"This article proposes that couples about to undertake marriage, as well as couples presently married, should be encouraged to discuss between themselves and with professional assistance the values and goals that each brings to the marriage, and the difficulties foreseen or already encountered in reconciling divergent ideas; it recommends that they be encouraged to reduce to writing a marriage contract by which they attempt to resolve these differences. We shall begin by detailing the proposal for a modern marriage contract, and then inquire into what the legal status of such a contract would be."

35. Francoeur, Anna K., and Robert T. Francoeur. *Hot and Cool Sex: Cultures in Conflict*; introduction by Robert H. Rimmer. New York: Harcourt Brace Jovanovich, 1974.

The authors examine, "within a religious and historical context, the changing sexual and marriage patterns in American society. . . . Employing Marshall McLuhan's terminology, the Francoeurs analyze the shift from the constraints and artificiality of 'hot' sex to the spontaneous enjoyment of 'cool sex.' . . . The time for drastic change in sexual relations is ripe, the Francoeurs believe. But the process is one of delicate balance." (Publisher)

36. Friedan, Betty. *The Feminine Mystique*. New York : W. W. Norton & Co., 1963.

The author believes that America needs "a drastic reshaping of the cultural image of femininity that will permit women to reach maturity, identity, completeness of self, without conflict with sexual fulfillment."

37. Gilmartin, Brian G. "That Swinging Couple Down the Block." *Psychology Today*, February 1975, pp. 54 ff.

"Married couples who agree to explore other beds may mortify mainstream sensibilities, but they're not all that different from conventional folk. Income and education are a bit lower, and there's less personal commitment to church, relatives, politics. But the big difference is that swingers see a high-fidelity marriage as keeping extracurricular sex visible and casual, and saving true love for hearth and spouse." (Editor)

38. Glick, Paul C. *Some Recent Changes in Amer-*

ican Families. Current Population Reports, Special Studies, ser. P-23, no. 52 (Washington, D.C.: Government Printing Office, n.d.).

Some of the recent trends discussed in this analytic report are more delay in marriage, more divorce among upper socioeconomic groups, more single-parent families, and more variety in living arrangements. The author also offers some possible courses of action for improving family life in America.

39. Greenbaum, Henry. "Marriage, Family and Parenthood." *American Journal of Psychiatry* 130 (November 1973): 1262-65.

"The author discusses the recent attacks against marriage, family, and parenthood by some of the leaders of the Women's Liberation Movement. He points out that the difficulties that cause human suffering in these institutions are not intrinsic to them but are determined by the quality of the people involved in them. He believes there is a deep human need for marriage, family, and parenthood, which has its roots in the prolonged biological and psychological dependency of the human child. The conditions of personality development necessary for successful functioning in marriage, family, and parenthood are analyzed." (Editor)

40. Greenwald, Harold. "Marriage as a Non-Legal Voluntary Association." In *The Family in Search of a Future: Alternate Models for Moderns,* edited by Herbert A. Otto, pp. 51-56. New York: Appleton-Century-Crofts, 1970.

The author believes that in changing marriage to a free voluntary association, "people would stay together for the only reason that makes marriage really viable--because they wanted to. . . . [It] would also permit experimentation in varieties of family life which would possibly be more in keeping with the needs of many individuals for whom life-long monogamous marriage is unsuited."

41. Hall, Elizabeth, and Robert A. Poteete. "Do you Mary, and Anne, and Beverly, and Ruth, take these men . . . a conversation with Robert H. Rimmer." *Psychology Today*, January 1972, pp. 57 ff.

Rimmer "talks about sex for the young, bigamy, group marriage, and--his latest proposal--structured adultery." (Editor)

42. Hansel, Robert R. "The Homosexual Problem . . . Theirs or Ours." New York: Section for Experimental and Specialized Services, Executive Council of the Episcopal Church, 1970.

"The principal material in [this] paper is from a research survey on attitudes and actions of Episcopalians regarding homosexuality. The purpose of the survey was to hold a mirror before the face of the church--a mirror in which the church might see its own responses to this pervasive form of sexual behavior."

43. Harris, Sophie. "The Impact of Changing Lifestyles on a Family Service Agency." *Journal of Jewish Communal Service* 52 (Spring 1976): 249-58.

The author describes a seminar set up by her agency "to look at various aspects of changing social patterns in [its] Jewish community. [The] seminar explored three areas: 1. Effect on practice of changing social patterns; 2. Workers' values regarding variant life styles; 3. Agency's need and readiness to change its image in the Jewish community."

44. Hendin, Herbert. *The Age of Sensation: A Psychoanalytic Exploration*. New York: W. W. Norton & Co., 1975.

"A psychoanalyst's portrait of the quality of emotional life in America, and of the forces which are operating in this culture to transform the young. . . . The outgrowth of a six year research project, . . . [it is] the first psychoanalytic study to base its findings primarily on non-patients selected at random." (Publisher)

45. Henze, Lura F., and John W. Hudson. "Personal and Family Characteristics of Cohabiting and Noncohabiting College Students." *Journal of Marriage and the Family* 36 (November 1974): 722-27.

For this study, "data were gathered in interviews with a random sample of 291 students at Arizona State University in 1971-72. The data indicated that 29 per cent of the males and 18 per cent of the females were currently cohabiting or had cohabited. Family characteristics examined failed to differentiate between cohabiters and noncohabiters. Personal characteristics which tended to distinguish the two groups were in the areas of religion, life style, and drug use. Cohabiters, compared to noncohabiters, were less apt to attend church, were more likely to identify with a liberal life style, and were more apt to be drug users."

46. Hoffman, Martin. *The Gay World: Male Homosexuality and the Social Creation of Evil*. New York: Basic Books, 1968.

A study of the "gay world--its character, its internal structure, and the problems which are generic to it." The author, a social psychiatrist, had been "engaged in a scientific study of the male homosexual community in the San Francisco Bay Area, under a grant from the National Institute of Mental Health." Intended for an audience of interested laymen.

47. Houriet, Robert. *Getting Back Together*. New York: Coward, McGann & Geoghegan, 1971.

For a year, the author traveled throughout America to explore "the texture and direction of communal life." Everywhere, he found "instability, transiency." But he also "discovered a new seriousness and commitment on the part of these 'unlikely pioneers' to forging alternative life-styles and to making them work." (Publisher) Told in first-person, diary style.

48. Hunt, Morton. *The Affair: A Portrait of Extra-Marital Love in Contemporary America*. New York: World Publishing Co., 1969.

In this book, the author tries "to describe the major types of extra-marital affair in contemporary America as [he] learned about them from people [he] interviewed or to whom [he] sent questionnaires. From their stories, it became clear to [him] that different kinds of affairs interact with different kinds of marriage in patterned ways--some extremely damaging to the marriages, others relatively innocuous, and still others distinctly beneficial. . . . [His] major aim has been to record and re-create a series of significant extra-marital experiences, and to make it possible for the reader to share the lives of other people and vicariously feel what they felt."

49. ———. *Sexual Behavior in the 1970's*. New York: Dell, 1975, c1974.

First published by Playboy Press in 1974. "Using detailed questionaires and in-depth interviews," this book "charts the changes in American attitudes and behavior in the wake of the sexual revolution." (Publisher)

50. Johnston, Charles M., and Robert W. Deisher. "Contemporary Communal Child Rearing: A First Analysis." *Mental Health Digest* 5, no. 10 (October 1973): 17-20.

This is a condensation of an article that appeared in *Pediatrics* (52 [1973]: 319-26) giving observations made by a medical student at twenty communes.

51. Kadushin, Alfred. "Single-Parent Adoptions: An Overview and Some Relevant Research." *The Social Service Review* 44 (September 1970): 263-74.

"This article reviews the problems and advantages of single-parent adoptions. It details the limited agency experience with such adoptions, the agency eligibility requirements in such adoptions, and the rationale for such requirements. It is noted that a principal deterrent to agency acceptance of such a procedure is the supposition that single parenthood is necessarily pathological. A review of relevant research is presented suggesting that the single-parent family is merely a variant child-rearing context and not inherently or necessarily pathogenic."

52. Kanter, Rosabeth Moss. "Communes." *Psychology Today*, July 1970, pp. 53 ff.

The author "studied 19th-Century American

communities, comparing 21 that lasted with nine that didn't, and . . . gathered information from 20 contemporary communes and from growth-and-learning communities. [She] then compared successful 19th-Century utopias and growth-center communities and found that while the growth centers tend to incorporate important features of the 19th-Century groups that were successful, many of the anarchist communes do not."

53. Kassel, Victor, "Polygyny After Sixty." In *The Family in Search of a Future: Alternate Models for Moderns,* edited by Herbert A. Otto, pp. 137-43. New York: Appleton-Century-Crofts, 1970.

"Polygyny after sixty is offered for consideration as a solution to a number of the social problems of the aged."

54. Keller, Suzanne. "Does the Family Have a Future?" *Journal of Comparative Family Studies* 2 (Spring 1971): 1-14.

A sociologist discusses fallacies currently held about the family, challenges to it, and the revolution in biology. She expects "some basic and irreversible changes in the decades ahead and the emergence of some novel forms of human togetherness."

55. Kempler, Hyman L. "Extended Kinship Ties and Some Modern Alternatives." *The Family Coordinator* 25 (April 1976): 143-49.

"The author contends that close relationships with extended kin have provided the nuclear family psychological and instrumental support, role models for the adult years, and a sense of historical continuity and perspective. With the waning of kin ties among a portion of today's middle class families, alternative family structures have arisen. Three of these--family networks, communes and the affiliated family--are critically evaluated with respect to their potential utility as substitutes for kin ties."

56. Kinkade, Kathleen. "Commune: A Walden-Two Experiment." *Psychology Today*, January 1973, pp. 35 ff.; February 1973, pp. 71 ff.

A personal account, in two parts, of communal life at Twin Oaks, a community established in 1967 on lines laid down by B. F. Skinner.

57. Kirkendall, Lester A., and Robert N. Whitehurst, eds. *The New Sexual Revolution;* with a preface by Paul Kurtz. New York: Donald W. Brown, 1971. (Distributed by Charles Scribner's Sons)

This book of readings includes the following: "American Sexophobia," by Robert N. Whitehurst; "Cross-Cultural Sexual Practices," by Herb Seal; "Evolving Sexual Ethics Within a Democratic Society," by Wesley J. Adams; "A Rational Sexual Morality," by Albert Ellis; "Sex Research," by Leon Salzman; "An Appraisal of Erotic Emotion and Autoerotic Behavior," by Walter R. Stokes; "The Homosexual Revolution--A Status Report," by Donald J. Cantor; "A Neuter and Desexualized Society?" by Charles Winick; "On Obscenity and Pornography," by Edward Sagarin; "Sex, Society and the Single Woman," by Luther G. Baker, Jr.; "Is Monogamy Outdated?" by Rustum and Della Roy; "Developing Human Sexuality," by Lester A. Kirkendall; "Youth and the Search for Intimacy," by Winfield W. and Frances F. Salisbury; "Contraception In and Out of Marriage," by Edward Pohlman; "Population Control and Personal Freedom--

Are They Compatible?" by Alice Taylor Day; "Sterilization--Accepting the Irrevocable," by Garrett Hardin.

58. Klaich, Dorothy. *Woman and Woman: Attitudes Toward Lesbianism*. New York: Simon and Schuster, 1974.

"Part I of this book outlines some of the sexual, medical, psychological, and purely scientific research that has been conducted in the field of female homosexuality. . . . Part II discusses the lives and times of some of the more articulate historical figures [who were lesbians]. . . . Part III allows some present-day lesbians to bear witness through the vehicle of anonymous questionnaires."

59. Klein, Carole. *The Single Parent Experience*. New York: Walker and Co., 1973.

Partial contents: "The Single Parent--Male," "Who Are the Unmarried Mothers of Today?" "Homosexual Parents," "Natural Motherhood," "The Single Parent's Family," "Child Care," "The Social Realities of Being a Single Parent," "The Alternative Life-Style," "The Psychological Effects of Having a Single Parent."

60. Knapp, Jacquelyn J. "Some Non-Monogamous Marriage Styles and Related Attitudes and Practices of Marriage Counselors." *The Family Coordinator* 24 (October 1975): 505-14.

"Four hundred sixty-five questionnaires were sent to a national random sample of the clinical membership of the American Association of Marriage and Family Counselors to ascertain their attitudes and practices toward clients involved in sexually open marriage, secret affairs, and recreational swinging. Counselors' biases toward such clients' behavior and personalities and variables associated with the biases are discussed, along with suggestions for couples seeking formal counseling or other options. Approaches for raising the consciousness of therapists about the effects of their personal values on professional treatment of clients with sexually non-traditional marriages are also considered."

61. Lake, Alice. "Childbirth in America." *McCall's*, January 1976, pp. 83 ff.

    Many American women "are now shopping around, before they choose an obstetrician and a hospital. Some, in full revolt, are bearing their children at home without professional aid. Others are using nurse-midwives instead of doctors to deliver their babies. A new concept--family centered childbirth--has been developed."

62. Lanes, Selma G. "Communes: A Firsthand Report on a Controversial New Life Style." *Parents' Magazine*, October 1971, pp. 61 ff.

    A middle-aged, middle-class mother provides her impressions of several communes that she visited.

63. LeShan, Eda J. "Mates and Roommates: New Styles in Young Marriages." New York: Public Affairs Committee, 1971.

    The author believes that "if a marriage takes place in order to legalize sex, it's in trouble: if living together is for sex without strings, it is also in trouble. But where genuine affection and responsible caring are as basic to the unmarried relationship as to the married, it may well be that young people can grow toward permanent emotional commitment through experimenting with one or several trial relationships." She also discusses the role of parents in helping their young people to discover their own roads to a gratifying life.

64. Levett, Carl. "A Parental Presence in Future Family Models." In *The Family in Search of a Future: Alternate Models for Moderns*, edited by Herbert A. Otto, pp. 161-69. New York: Appleton-Century-Crofts, 1970.

"With paternal figures in diminishing supply," Levett believes that "greater use will need to be made of supplementary masculine resources to close the father-son guidance gap. . . . The trend toward specialization of skills and talents will make possible the emergence of a 'third parent,' a male figure educated, trained, and equipped to serve the socializing needs of male children." He goes on to describe the possible role and activities of a third parent.

65. Levine, Saul V.; Robert P. Carr; and Wendy Horenblas. "The Urban Commune: Fact or Fad, Promise or Pipedream?" *American Journal of Orthopsychiatry* 43 (January 1973): 149-63.

The authors studied thirty communes located in urban centers and "looked at a wide range of issues, including members' backgrounds, motivation for joining, extent of sharing, sex and love, drugs, group decisions and process, change over time, and ideology. Factors predisposing to success or failure and implications for our society are discussed."

66. Libby, Roger W., and Robert N. Whitehurst, eds. *Renovating Marriage*. Danville, Calif.: Consensus Publishers, 1973.

The book of readings is divided into four

topical sections. They are "The State of Sex and Monogamy," "Sexual Freedom for Whom?" "Views of Future Participants," and "Marriage: Emergent Futures." Revised edition, entitled *Marriage and Alternatives: Exploring Intimate Relationships*, will be published by Scott, Foresman and Company in October 1976.

67. Lipman-Blumen, Jean. "The Implications for Family Structure of Changing Sex Roles." *Social Casework* 57 (February 1976): 67-79.

    "National demographic trends are coupled with other socioeconomic factors to predict family, occupational, and social structure during the next two decades." (Editor)

68. Lyness, Judith L.; Milton E. Lipetz; and Keith E. Davis. "Living Together: An Alternative to Marriage." *Journal of Marriage and the Family* 34 (May 1972): 305-11.

    "Questionnaire data on interpersonal feelings and social background variables were obtained from 31 going-together couples and 18 living-together couples. . . . It was found that the going-together couples held traditional orientations toward each other with commitment to marriage forming a strong part of this orientation. The living-together couples appeared to come to their arrangement with varied expectations."

69. Mace, David R. "The Sexual Revolution: Its Impact on Pastoral Care and Counseling." *Journal of Pastoral Care* 25 (December 1971): 220-32.

    The author believes that the sexual revolution is over. He discusses "a variety of areas of human sexuality in which difficulties requiring pastoral care and counseling frequently arise." Among these are sex education, masturbation, homosexuality, premarital intercourse, extramarital intercourse, marital-sexual adjustment, sexual deviations, abortion, and sexuality in the later years.

70. ———, ed. "Marriage Enrichment." *The Family Coordinator* 24 (April 1975): 131-73.

The special section contains the following articles: "Marriage Enrichment--Wave of the Future?" by David R. and Vera C. Mace; "Marriage and Family Enrichment Programs in North America--Report and Analysis," by Herbert A. Otto; "Recent Progress in Understanding and Facilitating Marital Communication," by Sherod Miller, Ramon Corrales, and Daniel B. Wackman; "Marriage Encounter: What Makes It Work?" by Ronald R. Regula; "The Pairing Enrichment Program: Actualizing the Marriage," by Robert P. and Patricia Y. Travis; "MARDILAB: An Experiment in Marriage Enrichment," by Edward V. Stein; and "Marriage Enrichment Concepts for Research," by David R. Mace.

71. ——— and Vera Mace. *We Can Have Better Marriages If We Really Want Them.* Nashville: Abingdon Press, 1974.

This book "offers a hopeful, positive view of marriage" and a plan "for building better marriages" through "marriage enrichment groups in which couples grow and learn together, helping and supporting one another." (Publisher)

72. Macklin, Eleanor D. "Heterosexual Cohabitation Among Unmarried College Students." *The Family Coordinator* 21 (October 1972): 463-72.

"This article is an initial exploration of unmarried cohabitation as experienced by female students at Cornell University, and includes a description of the nature of the relationship, the reasons for involvement, and attendant problems and benefits. Discussion is based on intensive interviews with fifteen junior and senior women, and questionnaire responses from 29 junior and senior women, all of whom had experienced cohabitation. The author suggests that living together unmarried is becoming an increasingly common aspect of campus courtship and is frequently associated with the 'going steady' phase of the dating relationship. Implications for research and education are indicated."

73. Margolis, Vera S. "Today's Jewish Woman: The Challenge of Change." *Journal of Jewish Communal Service* 52 (Winter 1975): 145-52.

The author suggests a "few important social changes which have had an impact on the way the contemporary woman leads her life and therefore on the many ways that family life is inexorably changed."

74. Mazur, Ronald. *The New Intimacy: Open-Ended Marriage and Alternate Lifestyles*. Boston: Beacon Press, 1973.

"The intent of the author is to point out some of the intricacies of open-end marriages, and other aspects of different lifestyles. He recognizes there is no 'support system' for these alternate styles, and says, 'This book, in fact, is written to change that abysmal situation.'" (Lester A. Kirkendall, *Journal of Marriage and the Family*)

75. Mead, Margaret. "Marriage in Two Steps." *Redbook Magazine*, July 1966, pp. 48 ff.

Also in *The Family in Search of a Future: Alternate Models for Moderns,* edited by Herbert A. Otto, pp. 75-84. New York: Appleton-Century-Crofts, 1970.

The author believes that "we need two types of marriage, one of which can (though it need not) develop into the other, each with its own possibilities and special responsibility. The first type of marriage may be called an individual marriage, binding together two individuals only. . . . As the first step in marriage, it would not include having children. In contrast, the second type of marriage, which I think of as a parental marriage, would be explicitly directed toward the founding of a family."

76. Miller, Emily. "Treatment of a Communal Family." *Social Casework* 54 (June 1973): 331-41.

"Viewing a new form of family life as a developmental milestone rather than as evidence of pathology leads to engaging parents and son in therapy." (Editor)

77. Millett, Kate. *Sexual Politics*. Garden City, N.Y.: Doubleday & Co., 1970.

The author proposes that "sex has a frequently neglected political aspect." She illustrates by "analyzing the social relationship between the sexes from a theoretical standpoint . . . [and] attempts to formulate a systematic overview of patriarchy as a political institution, . . . outlining the great transformation in the traditional relationship between the sexes which took place in the nineteenth and early twentieth centuries, and then giving an account of the climate of reaction which later set in, assuring the continuation of a modified patriarchal way of life, and frustrating the possibility of revolutionary social change in this area for some three decades." The book closes with a focus upon the work of several significant literary figures of recent times--D. H. Lawrence, Henry Miller, Norman Mailer, and Jean Genêt.

78. Movius, Margaret. "Voluntary Childlessness--the Ultimate Liberation." *The Family Coordinator* 25 (January 1976): 57-63.

"Working mothers experience tremendous demands on their time and energy as a result of the combined responsibilities of a job, a family, and a home. Career-oriented wives may increasingly consider the child-free state as a liberating alternative. Freed from child care responsibilities, a woman who is committed to a career may benefit from greater mobility, fewer family commitments, and more time for professional development. Career women may find the flexibility and freedom afforded them by the child-free alternative are necessary for competing in today's world."

79. National Institute of Mental Health. *Parents Are People, Too*. Rockville, Md.: U.S. Department of Health, Education, and Welfare, 1975. Publication no. 017-024-00482-1. (Available for sale from the U.S. Government Printing Office.)

In preparing this booklet, we have attempted to gather information about community resources upon which parents can draw to strengthen and enrich their lives. The programs described are not for parents with serious problems, nor for families already in trouble. The programs are educational and preventive in nature. Their goal is to enhance the capabilities and personal development of individuals in the many aspects of their lives as parents and as people."

80. Neubeck, Gerhard, ed. *Extra-marital Relations*. Englewood Cliffs, N.J.: Prentice-Hall, 1969.

In this volume, "the editor and nine other contributors, including sexologists, sociologists, and psychologists, . . . explore the causes, varieties, and results of extra-marital relations."

81. Novak, Michael. "The Family Out of Favor." *Harper's Magazine,* April 1976, pp. 37-40 ff.

The author believes that "the courage to marry and raise children presupposes a willingness (presently unfashionable) to grow up."

82. Ogg, Elizabeth. *Homosexuality in Our Society*. New York: Public Affairs Committee, 1972. (Public Affairs Pamphlet no. 484)

The author gives a brief history of male homosexuality and discusses the suggested possible causes of homosexuality, myths and stereotypes regarding the male homosexual, and his rights under the law. She also discusses the plight of the lesbian.

83. Olson, David H. "Marriage of the Future: Revolutionary or Evolutionary Change?" *The Family Coordinator* 21 (October 1972): 383-93.

"This paper describes some of the evolutionary changes that are taking place in the institutions of marriage and the family, none of which are truly revolutionary in the sense that they will destroy the institutions in the near future. The paper also explores the dating-mating game, the numerous myths which relate to marriage, the changing sexual patterns in our society, and the alternative styles of living that are presently being tried by some individuals. Recommendations are made regarding several issues related to hopefully improving marriage and family relationships."

84. O'Neill, Nena, and George O'Neill. "Open Marriage: Implications for Human Service Systems." *The Family Coordinator* 22 (October 1973): 449-56.

"The authors of *Open Marriage* reiterate the meaning and possibilities of the open marriage concept and advance suggestions for change in the areas of residence, work, child care, and educational patterns. Human service systems must search out the universal values to be maintained in all human relationships."

85. Osmond, Humphry; Violet Franks; and Vasanti Burtle. "Changing Views of Women and Therapeutic Approaches: Some Historical Considerations." In *Women in Therapy: New Psychotherapies for a Changing Society*, edited by Violet Franks and Vasanti Burtle, pp. 3-24. New York: Brunner/Mazel, 1974.

In this chapter, the authors provide "some hints and indications suggesting the importance of the historical background to current psychiatric treatment for women, as well as to those activities usually subsumed under the heading of psychotherapy."

86. Otto, Herbert A., ed. *The Family in Search of a Future: Alternate Models for Moderns.* New York: Appleton-Century-Crofts, 1970.

Partial contents: "Alternate Models from the Perspective of Sociology,"* by John F. Cuber; "An Alternate Model from a Theological Perspective," by Edward C. Hobbs; "Reinventing Marriage: The Perspective of a Psychologist," by Sidney M. Jourard; "Marriage as a Non-legal Voluntary Association,"* by Harold Greenwald; "Marriage as a Human-Actualizing Contract,"* by Virginia Satir; "Progressive Monogamy: An Alternate Pattern?"* by Ethel Alpenfels; "Marriage in Two Steps,"* by Margaret Mead; "Group Marriage: A Possible Alternative?" by Albert Ellis; "Polyandry and Polygyny: Viable Today?" by Gerhard Neubeck; "The New Marriage: Marriage as a Framework for Developing Personal Potential," by Herbert A. Otto; "The Tribal Family and the Society of Awakening," by Joseph J. Downing; "Polygyny after Sixty,"* by Victor Kassel; "The Intimate Network of Families as a New Structure,"* by Frederick H. Stoller; "A Parental Presence in Future Family Models,"* by Carl Levett; "Implications of New Models of the Family for the Aging Population," by George Rosenberg; "List of Growth Centers and Organizations for Actualizing Human Potential."

*There is a separate listing in this bibliography for this article.

87. ——— , ed. *Marriage and Family Enrichment: New Perspectives and Programs*. Nashville: Abingdon Press, 1976.

Chapters in this book are: "Marriage and Family Enrichment Programs: An Overview of a Movement," by Herbert A. Otto; "The Family Growth Group: Guidelines for an Emerging Means of Strengthening Families," by Douglas A. Anderson; "The Family Enrichment Weekend," by Russell L. and June N. Wilson; "The Family Camp: An Extended Family Enrichment Experience," by Ed Branch, Jr.; "The Care-Lab: A Family Enrichment Program," by Kenneth G. Prunty; "The Family

Home Evening: A National Ongoing Family Enrichment Program," by Au-Deane S. Cowley and Ramona S. Adams; "A Christian Marriage Enrichment Retreat," by Herbert Green, Jr.; "Marriage Encounter: An Ecumenical Enrichment Program," by Antoinette Bosco; "The More Joy in Your Marriage Program," by Herbert and Roberta Otto; "Marriage Renewal Retreats," by Abraham and Dorothy Schmitt; "Positive Partners: A Marriage Enrichment Communication Course," by Don Hayward; "The Jewish Marriage Encounter," by Bernard Kligfeld; "The Gestalt Perspective: A Marriage Enrichment Program," by Joseph C. Zinker and Julian P. Leon; "Transactional Analysis Tools for Use in Marriage Enrichment Programs," by Hedges and Betty Capers; "We Call It ACME," by David R. Mace; "The Minnesota Couples Communication Program," by Elam W. Nunnally, Sherod Miller, and Daniel B. Wackman; "The Marriage Enrichment Program--Phase I," by Del and Trudy Vander Haar; "The Phase II Marriage Enrichment Lab," by Bud and Bea Van Eck; "The Marriage Communication Labs," by Paul and LaDonna Hopkins; "Developing a National Marriage Communication Lab Training Program," by Leon and Antoinette Smith; "Cassette Programs for Training and Enrichment," by Howard J. Clinebell, Jr.

88. ———, ed. *The New Sexuality*. Palo Alto, Calif.: Science and Behavior Books, 1971.

Includes the following papers: "The New Sexuality: An Introduction," by Herbert A. Otto; "Sexuality as a Personal and Social Force," by Ben N. Ard, Jr.; "New Sex Findings: Some Trends and Implications,"* by Isadore Rubin; "Emotions and Sexuality in the Man," by LeMon Clark; "Emotions and Sexuality in the Woman," by Eleanor Hamilton; "Sex as a Regenerative Force," by Jessie

Bernard; "Sexual Adventuring and Personality Growth," by Albert Ellis; "Sensory Awakening and Sensuality," by Bernard Gunther; "Enhancing Sexuality Through Nudism," by William E. Hartman and Marilyn A. Fithian; "Sexual Life-styles and Fulfillments,"* by John F. Cuber; "Sex and Marital Enrichment," by David R. Mace; "Positive Values of the Affair," by O. Spurgeon English; "Sex as Fun," by Harold Greenwald; "The New Sexuality and the Homosexual," by Del Martin and Phyllis Lyon; "Sex and Health," by Joel Fort; "Sexuality: Rewards and Responsibilities," by Ethel M. Nash; "Control of Procreation: A New Dimension of Freedom," by Walter R. Stokes; "Premarital Sex from an Existential Perspective," by S. Jeffrey Garfield, Sander I. Marcus, and Elizabeth Garfield; "Sex and American Attitudes," by Robert A. Harper; "Sexuality--A Creative Force?" by Mary S. Calderone.

*There is a separate listing in this bibliography for this article.

89. Packard, Vance. *The Sexual Wilderness: The Contemporary Upheaval in Male-Female Relationships*. New York: David McKay Co., 1968.

Partial contents: "A New Environment for Sexual Awakening and Maturing," "The Shifting World of the Sexes," "Trends in Premarital Intimacy . . . ," "Changing Patterns in Mate-Seeking Behavior," "The Married Confrontation: Coping with Some Novel Patterns," "How the Future Might Look," "Possible Approaches for Sharing Amicably," "Possible Norms for Coping Agreeably with Our Sexuality," "On Improving the Prospects for Sound Marriages."

90. Peterson, Gail Beaton, and Larry R. Peterson. "Sexism in the Treatment of Sexual Dysfunction." *The Family Coordinator* 22 (October 1973): 397-404.

"Our study examines sexual roles in popular sex and marriage manuals, with particular attention to the suggested causes and aids for sexual problems. By reviewing popular books, we felt we could gain perspective on the attitudes and frameworks being 'sold' to the public. We found large differences in responsibility for sexual dysfunction between the sexes, with females seen more frequently as the 'cause' and 'cure' for the most common sexual problems."

91. Poll, Rosemary. "Group Marriage: An Alternate Lifestyle." *Canadian Welfare* 49 (September/October 1973): 15-17.

The author discusses the characteristics of group marriage, the Constantine studies of this alternate life-style, and the law and the attitudes of social workers insofar as group marriage is concerned.

92. Pringle, Bruce M. "Family Clusters as a Means of Reducing Isolation Among Urbanites." *The Family Coordinator* 23 (April 1974): 175-79.

"Many urban residents do not have the emotional support of an adequate network of kin, friends, or neighbors. It has been proposed that such persons might join together into artificial extended families or family clusters. About a dozen adults of various ages and marital statuses plus their children could agree to meet regularly to have fun together, share knowledge and skills, help each other in personal growth, and provide mutual support in joy and sorrow. Experiences in the formation and operation of a cluster are described on the basis of participant observation."

93. Ramey, James W. "Communes, Group Marriage and the Upper-Middle Class." *Journal of Marriage and the Family* 34 (November 1972): 647-55.

"An analysis of eighty couples' three-year exploration of the feasibility of entering into communal living or group marriage, based on interviews, questionnaires, discussion group notes, correspondence, and anecdotal records. Over 90 per cent of husbands and wives, if employed, were in academic, professional, or managerial positions."

94. ———. *Intimate Friendships.* Englewood Cliffs, N.J.: Prentice-Hall, 1976.

"Basing his discussion on current social and psychological findings, [the author] reviews many types of relationships from dating to group marriage. . . . [He] explores the pros and cons of different life-styles. He compares these alternatives to traditional marriage in terms of personal freedom and growth." (Publisher)

95. ———. "Intimate Networks: Will They Replace the Monogamous Family?" *The Futurist* 9 (August 1975): 175-81.

"A social scientist looks closely at [one alternative to traditional marriage]--the intimate network, a lifestyle that has only recently been clearly identified, named, and subjected to serious study." (Editor) Similar to traditional friendship, an intimate friendship, however, may include sexual activity.

96. Rice, Joy K., and David G. Rice. "Implications of the Women's Liberation Movement for Psychotherapy." *American Journal of Psychiatry* 130 (February 1973): 191-96.

"The authors examine the implications of the women's liberation movement for current psychotherapeutic theory and practice in terms of the antifeminine Freudian position, the predominance of male therapists, the concept of role unhappiness as psychopathological, and the threat to the therapist's social power. Consideration of role conflict in sociological terms instead of the intrapsychic rubric is especially emphasized. The authors also discuss related issues concerning the training of therapists and propose a model using male and female cotherapists." (Editor)

97. Rogers, Carl R. *Becoming Partners: Marriage and Its Alternatives*. New York: Delacorte Press, 1972.

This book is built around tape-recorded interviews with young couples who discuss their relationships. What the author appears to be saying is that the "days of the rigid, legalistic marriage are over and we are moving experimentally toward new forms which can achieve true partnership without violating selfhood." (*The Family Coordinator*)

98. Rosenberg, George. "Implications of New Models of the Family for the Aging Population." In *The Family in Search of a Future: Alternate Models for Moderns*, edited by Herbert A. Otto, pp. 171-81. New York: Appleton-Century-Crofts, 1970.

The author explores the possibility of polygynous marriage as a "solution to the problems of the bereft female in old age." He believes, however, that it "would tend to disrupt kinship relations and introduce an element of rigidity in the class system. And polygyny also would tend to divert the energies of old people from an important expressive role they play in integrating the family network."

99. Roy, Rustum, and Della Rustum. "Is Monogamy Outdated?" *The Humanist* 30, no. 2 (March/April 1970): 19-26.

The authors are convinced that "'traditional monogamy' as an ideal may be altered in a continuous fashion in order to respond to the needs of men and women today." They suggest institutionalizing premarital sex, expanding the erotic community in the post-marital years, and legalizing bigamy.

100. Rubin, Isadore. "New Sex Findings: Some Trends and Implications." In *The New Sexuality,* edited by Herbert A. Otto, pp. 26-43. Palo Alto, Calif.: Science and Behavior Books, 1971.

The author "has compiled a summary of recent findings from sex research and explores the implications and trends flowing from this work." (Editor)

101. Sands, Rosalind M. "Toward Communal Child Rearing." *Social Work* 18, no. 3 (May 1973): 54-59.

"Social work's preoccupation with the preservation of the nuclear family has blinded it to the necessity of finding new ways to care for children. This myopia has impeded recognition of the forces in American life that are bringing social change and new forms of child rearing. The author describes some of these phenomena and concludes that communal rearing must be seriously considered in this country."

102. Sanville, Jean, and Joel Shor. "Leading Ladies and Gentle Men: Some Clinical Clues to Transitional Phases in Husband-Wife Roles." *Clinical Social Work Journal* 1 (Summer 1973): 67-77.

"In this paper we offer some clinical examples to illustrate certain phases that we see occurring as new husband-wife roles emerge and new constellations evolve. With one exception, the patients we describe are white, middle-class Americans. . . . We would like to highlight some of the motives for change on the part of both men and women, some of the conflicts that are precipitated as a consequence of change, and some of the readjustments and solutions which are attempted. Finally, we would like to hazard some guesses about the long-range directions in which these changes seem to be headed."

103. Satir, Virginia. "Marriage as a Human-Actualizing Contract." In *The Family in Search of a Future: Alternate Models for Moderns*, edited by Herbert A. Otto, pp. 57-66. New York: Appleton-Century-Crofts, 1970.

The author presents "some ideas which might go a long way toward moving us all a notch forward in our whole human existence and consequently in the marriage relationship." Among these are changes in child-rearing practices, a trial period of living together for potential partners before their actual marriage, the removal of ignorance and secrecy about the sexual part of the human being, and establishment of neighborhood

Family Growth Centers "for learning about being human, from birth to death."

104. Seidenberg, Robert. "Moving On to What?" *MH* 59, no. 1 (Winter 1975): 6-11.

"Constant changes of community can mean enhancement for an ambitious husband, but for the dutiful wife who follows, they inevitably lead to an identity-shredded nightmare."

105. Sherman, Sanford N. "The Therapist and Changing Sex Roles." *Social Casework* 57 (February 1976): 93-96.

This article "highlights the interesting challenges currently presented to practitioners in family therapy." (Editor)

106. Shireman, Joan F., and Penny R. Johnson. "Single Persons as Adoptive Parents." *Social Service Review* 50 (March 1976): 103-16.

"This study, following a group of single parents for the first four years of their lives with adopted children, illustrates some of the satisfactions and problems of this form of adoption. The homes are diverse in family structure, income, and occupation, and in ability to meet the needs of the child. However, some distinctive family patterns can be identified. The study points to the need for more information about these adoptions in order to differentiate the applicant who will become the remarkably capable parent from the applicant whose child may later experience difficulties."

107. Silverman, Anna, and Arnold Silverman. *The Case Against Having Children*. New York: David McKay Co., 1971.

"Presents numerous arguments to support its contention that institutionalized parenthood is neither necessary nor beneficial for all and that it is, in fact, threatening our survival in today's pollution-plagued world. Written informally and nontechnically." (*Family Life Literature and Films: An Annotated Bibliography, 1972* [Minneapolis: Council on Family Relations, n.d.])

108. Smith, David E., and James Sternfield. "The Hippie Communal Movement: Effects on Child Birth and Development." *American Journal of Orthopsychiatry* 40 (April 1970): 527-30.

In discussing "the effect of the communal life style on childbirth and child development," the authors describe the significant characteristics of psychedelic communes and speculate upon their future.

109. Smith, James R., and Lynn G. Smith. *Beyond Monogamy: Recent Studies of Sexual Alternatives in Marriage*. Baltimore: Johns Hopkins University Press, 1974.

This is "a collection of sixteen articles and research reports whose contributors seek understanding of relatively new patterns and styles of marriage, including: co-marital sex, group marriage, 'swinging,' and related sexual practices." (Publisher) Articles included are: "Sexuality in a Zero Growth Society," by Alex Comfort; "Open Marriage: A Conceptual Framework," by Nena O'Neill and George O'Neill; "The Sociology of Mate Swapping," by Duane Denfeld and Michael Gordon; "Co-Marital Sex: The Incorporation of Extramarital Sex into the Marriage Relationship," by Lynn G. Smith and James R. Smith; "Emerging Patterns of Innovative Behavior in Marriage," by James W. Ramey; "Infidelity: Some Moral and Social Issues," by Jessie Bernard; "The Emergence of Middle-Class Deviant Subcultures: The Case of Swingers," by Mary Lindenstein Walshok; "Group Marriage: A Possible Alternative?" by Albert Ellis; "Group Sex Among the Mid-Americans," by Gilbert D. Bartell; "Co-Marital Sex and the Sexual Freedom Movement," by James R. Smith and Lynn G. Smith; "Communes, Group Marriage, and the Upper-Middle Class," by James W. Ramey; "Sexual Liberality and Personality: A Pilot Study," by Jon Twichell; "An Exploratory Study of Spouse Swapping," by Charles A. Varni; "Dropouts from Swinging: The Marriage Counselor as Informant," by Duane Denfeld; "Sexual Aspects of Multilateral Relations," by Larry L. Constantine and Joan M. Constantine; "Sexual Deviance and Social Networks: A Study of Social, Family, and Marital Interaction Patterns among Co-Marital Sex Participants," by Brian G. Gilmartin.

110. "Special Report: The Future of Women and Marriage." *The Futurist* 4, no. 2 (April 1970).

Includes the following articles: "Women, Marriage and the Future," by Jessie Bernard; "Will Women Become Counterfeit Men?" by Mary I. Hooker; "Where Is Marriage Going?" by Larry and Joan Constantine; "The Prophet of Group Marriage," by William T. Gay; "The Future of the Family," by Myron Orleans and Florence Wolfson; "Living Together: An Alternative to Marriage," by Theodora Wells with Lee S. Christie; "The Volita Project, or Can Technology Replace Women?" by Victor J. Papanek.

111. Speck, Ross V., with Jean Barr et al. *The*

New Families: Youth, Communes, and the Politics of Drugs. New York: Basic Books, 1972.

The author, with a multidisciplinary team, "visited dozens of youth communes, in an effort to understand them and what their members are trying to achieve. Out of his investigations there emerges a picture of commune life . . . --the daily activities, the sexual patterns, the role of women, the variety of household arrangements, and, especially, the use of drugs. . . ." (Publisher)

112. ——— and Joan Speck. "The Urban Commune--An Alternative Family Style: Implications for Family Therapists." *Family Therapy* 2, no. 2 (1975): 181-86.

The authors discuss changes in American communes since the early 1960s along with their experiences in treating communal units. They believe it is time for family therapists to give their "accumulated knowledge, experience, and dedication, from depth psychology to general systems, to those human beings, mostly younger than . . . [they] who are trying to forge a new humanity [through development of forms of family innovation]."

113. Stein, Peter J. "Singlehood: An Alternative to Marriage." *The Family Coordinator* 24 (October 1975): 489-503.

This paper "analyzes singlehood as a positive choice made by adults who have chosen not to marry or re-marry. Census data and surveys indicate the increasing postponement of marriage and the growing number of singles in the United States. Twenty in-depth interviews with single men and women reveal a complex set of experiences surrounding the decision to remain single. Despite cultural and psychological pressures toward marriage and discriminatory social practices, respondents testified to personal growth, an increase in opportunities and friendships, and a sense of independence that validated their present lifestyles. Correlatively, the growth of interpersonal support structures for singles and an emergent ideology of singlehood are identified."

114. Stoller, Frederick. "The Intimate Network of Families as a New Structure." In *The Family in Search of a Future: Alternate Models for Moderns*, edited by Herbert A. Otto, pp. 145-59. New York: Appleton-Century-Crofts, 1970.

"The increasing mobility of the American family creates greater isolation from the extended family. . . . Limiting rather than enhancing, the isolated family tends to become more rigid and impoverished in terms of the influence, satisfaction and ritual generated. An alternative structure is seen in the intimate network of families, in which three or four families come together on a regular basis to explore their living arrangements, to exchange intimacies, to provide services for one another, and to develop new and more realistic, and more exciting, systems of values and attitudes."

115. Streib, Gordon F., ed. *The Changing Family: Adaptation and Diversity*. Reading, Mass.: Addison-Wesley Publishing Co., 1973.

This anthology contains the following articles: "What Is the Future of Marriage," by Judy Nicol, Pat Novik-Raby, and Francis

L. Filas; "Revolution in Sex Behavior," by Pitirim A. Sorokin; "The Family Is Out of Fashion," by Ann Richardson Roiphe; "Marriage and the Nuclear Family as Target," by Jessie Bernard; "Parents Without Partners," by E. E. LeMasters; "Five Kinds of Relationships," by John F. Cuber and Peggy B. Harroff; "Group Marriage: A Possible Alternative?" by Albert Ellis; "The Swingers," by Duane Denfeld and Michael Gordon; "The Family in Collective Settlements in Israel," by Y. Talmon-Garber; "Communal Living: Economic Survival and Family Life," by Joyce Gardener; "Dropping Out in Manhattan: An Experiment in Middle-Class Fantasy," by Colette Dowling; "Prospects for Change in American Sexual Patterns," by John H. Gagnon and William Simon; "Facts and Forecasts about the Family and Old Age," by Gordon F. Streib; "North American Marriage: 1990,"* by Leo Davids.

*There is a separate listing in this bibliography for this article.

116. Sussman, Marvin B. "Family Systems in the 1970's: Analysis, Policies, and Programs." *The Annals of the American Academy of Political and Social Science*, 396 (July 1971): 40-56.

"This paper contains a brief review of some of the salient discoveries and theoretical formulations which provide the most powerful explanations of the issues and problems faced by different types of families in their dealings with institutional systems and bureaucratic organizations. Specifically covered are variant family forms, structural properties of kin family systems, family/organizational linkages, major tasks and functions of families, the kin network as a mediating-linking system, and changes in the internal role structure of the family. The second section deals with practical applications, needed policies, programs, and strategies for increasing the level of competence of human service systems to meet the expectations, capabilities, interests, and aspirations of members of variant family forms found in pluralistic societies."

117. ——— , ed. *Non-Traditional Family Forms in the 1970's*. Minneapolis: National Council on Family Relations, 1972.

The articles in this book were orginally published in the October 1972 issue (volume 21) of *The Family Coordinator*. They include: "The Meaning of Variant and Experimental Marriage Styles and Family Forms in the 1970's," by Marvin B. Sussman and Betty E. Cogswell; "Marriage of the Future: Revolutionary or Evolutionary Change?"* by David H. Olson; "Some Comparisons of Conventional and Counterculture Families," by Robert N. Whitehurst; "Open Marriage: A Synergic Model," by Nena O'Neill and George O'Neill; "Androgyny as a Life Style,"* by Joy D. Osofsky and Howard J. Osofsky; "The Communal Family," by Bennett Berger, Bruce Hackett, and R. Mervyn Millar; "Ethical and Ideological Problems for Communal Living: A Caveat," by Joy G. Schulterbrandt and Edwin J. Nichols; "Emerging Patterns of Innovative Behavior in Marriage," by James W. Ramey; "Dissolution of Marriage in a Nonconventional Context," by Larry L. Constantine and Joan M. Constantine; "Heterosexual Cohabitation Among Unmarried College Students,"* by Eleanor D. Macklin; "Sister Love: An Exploration of the Need for Homosexual Experience," by Janis Kelly; "Comparative Life Styles and Family and Friend

Relationships Among Older Black Women," by Jacquelyne Johnson Jackson; "The Future of Family Relationships in the Middle and Older Years: Clues in Fiction," by Rose M. Somerville; "The Affiliated Family: A Continued Analysis," by Sylvia Clavan and Ethel Vatter; and "Changing Family and Marriage Forms: Complications for Human Service Systems,"* by Betty E. Cogswell and Marvin B. Sussman.

*There is a separate listing in this bibliography for this article.

118. ——— , ed. "The Second Experience: Variant Family Forms and Life Styles." *The Family Coordinator* 24 (October 1975): 391-576.

Articles included in this special issue are: "Variant Family Forms and Life Styles: Rejection of the Traditional Nuclear Family," by Betty E. Cogswell; "Variant Family Forms in a World Perspective," by Teresa Donati Marciano; "Men, Women, and Equity," by Rhona Rapoport and Robert N. Rapoport; "Coupling, Parenting, and the Presence of Others: Intimate Relationships in Communal Households," by Rosabeth Moss Kanter, Dennis Jaffe, and D. Kelly Weisberg; "An Analysis of Communes and Intentional Communities with Particular Attention to Sexual and Genderal Relations," by Patrick W. Conover; "Beyond Equality of the Sexes: The Question of the Children," by Judith Lorber; "The Moral Careers of Voluntarily Childless Wives: Notes on the Defense of a Variant World View,"* by J. E. Veevers; "Singlehood: An Alternative to Marriage,"* by Peter J. Stein; "Some Non-Monogamous Marriage Styles and Related Attitudes and Practices of Marriage Counselors,"* by Jacquelyn J. Knapp; "Intimate Groups and Networks: Frequent Consequences of Sexually Open Marriage," by James W. Ramey; "To Love, Honor, and Obey? Traditional Legal Marriage and Alternative Family Forms," by Lenore J. Weitzman; "Alternative Family Structures and the Law," by D. Kelly Weisberg; "Family Synergy, A Variant Family Organization," by Patrick LaFollette; "The Four F's of Variant Family Forms and Marriage Styles," by Marvin B. Sussman.

*There is a separate listing in this bibliography for this article.

119. Toffler, Alvin. "The Fractured Family." In *Future Shock*, pp. 211-30. New York: Random House, 1970.

The author believes that "the family may neither vanish nor enter upon a new Golden Age. It may--and this is far more likely--break up, shatter, only to come together in weird and novel ways." He discusses the probable impact of the new birth technology, "childless marriage, professional parenthood, post-retirement childrearing, corporate families, communes, geriatric group marriages, homosexual family units [and] polygamy."

120. Veevers, J. E. "The Child-Free Alternative: Rejection of the Motherhood Mystique." In *Women in Canada*, edited by Marylee Stephenson, pp. 183-99. Toronto: New Press, 1973.

"Over the past several years, the phenomenon of voluntary childlessness in Canada has been subjected to preliminary study. This paper is concerned with the presentation of some of the findings of this research."

121. ———. "The Moral Careers of Voluntarily Childless Wives: Notes on the Defense of a Variant World View." *The Family Coordinator* 24 (October 1975): 473-87.

"Although voluntarily childless couples perceive that their antinatalist sentiments result in a variety of negative sanctions, they remain relatively unperturbed by social pressure. This paradoxical situation is achieved and maintained through adherence to a variant world view which is essentially the obverse of the motherhood mystique. Four related defense mechanisms are involved and discussed by the author. . . . Several conditions are outlined which may maximize the viability of voluntary childlessness as an alternative to traditional family forms."

122. Veysey, Laurence. "Communal Sex and Communal Survival: Individualism Busts the Commune Boom." *Psychology Today,* December 1974, pp. 73-78.

The author compares "various group sexual arrangements of today's social experiments with those of 19th-century American communes."

123. Wells, J. Gipson. "A Critical Look at Personal Marriage Contracts." *The Family Coordinator* 25 (January 1976): 33-37.

"Personal marriage contracts are subjected to critical analysis and evaluation with particular emphasis on negative aspects and consequences often overlooked by popular treatments of this topic. Some of these are: questionable legality, inability to anticipate real problems in marriage, attitude changes after marriage, lack of flexibility, and the pessimistic outlook reflected in these contracts. Some positive considerations are also offered, along with suggestions for improvements in the use of premarriage contracts."

124. Winberg, M. S., and C. J. Williams. *Male Homosexuals: Their Problems and Adaptations*. New York: Oxford University Press, 1974.

"This empirical cross-cultural study of homosexuality stresses the importance of social adaptation as a central theory in understanding the homosexual." (*The Family Coordinator*)

125. "The Women's Movement." *American Journal of Orthopsychiatry* 41 (October 1971): 708-92.

Some of the articles included in this special section are: "Changing the Role of Women," by Mordeca Jane Pollock; "Changes in the Modern Family: Their Impact on Sex Roles," by Janet Zollinger Giele; "Psychological Consequences of Sexual Inequality," by Jean Baker Miller and Ira Mothner; "The Single Woman in Today's Society: A Reappraisal,"* by Margaret Adams.

*There is a separate listing in this bibliography for this article.

DIRECTORY OF PUBLISHERS AND SOURCES OF MATERIALS LISTED IN BIBLIOGRAPHY

Abingdon Press, 201 Eighth Avenue South, Nashville, Tenn. 37202

Addison-Wesley Publishing Company, Jacob Way, Reading, Mass. 01867

American Journal of Orthopsychiatry, 1775 Broadway, New York, N.Y. 10019

The American Journal of Psychiatry, 1700 Eighteenth Street, N.W., Washington, D.C. 20009

The Annals of the American Academy of Political and Social Science, 3937 Chestnut Street, Philadelphia, Pa. 19104

Appleton-Century-Crofts, Route 9W, Englewood Cliffs, N.J. 07632

Association Press, 291 Broadway, New York, N.Y. 10007

Bantam Books, 666 Fifth Avenue, New York, N.Y. 10019

Basic Books, 10 East Fifty-third Street, New York, N.Y. 10022

Beacon Press, 25 Beacon Street, Boston, Mass. 02108

William C. Brown, Publishers, 2460 Kerper Boulevard, Dubuque, Iowa 52001

Brunner/Mazel, 64 University Place, New York, N.Y. 10003

Canadian Welfare, 55 Parkdale Avenue, Box 3505, Station C, Ottawa, Ontario, Canada K1Y 4G1

Clinical Social Work, Business Office, Human Sciences Press, 72 Fifth Avenue, New York, N.Y. 10011

Consensus Publishers, 155 Franciscan Drive, San Ramon, Calif. 94583

Coward, McCann & Geoghegan, 200 Madison Avenue, New York, N.Y. 10016

Delacorte Press, 1 Dag Hammarskjold Plaza (245 East Forty-seventh Street), New York, N.Y. 10017

Dell Publishing Company, 1 Dag Hammarskjold Plaza (245 East Forty-seventh Street), New York, N.Y. 10017

Dial Press, 1 Dag Hammarskjold Plaza (245 East Forty-seventh Street), New York, N.Y. 10017

Doubleday & Company, 245 Park Avenue, New York, N.Y. 10017

Executive Council of the Episcopal Church, 815 Second Avenue, New York, N.Y. 10017

The Family Coordinator, 1219 University Avenue, S.E., Minneapolis, Minn. 55414

Family Law Quarterly, 1155 East Sixtieth Street, Chicago, Ill. 60637

Family Process, 149 East Seventy-eighth Street, New York, N.Y. 10021

Family Service Association of America, 44 East Twenty-third Street, New York, N.Y. 10010

Family Therapy, Libra Publishers, 391 Willets Road, P.O. Box 165, Roslyn Heights, N.Y. 11577

The Futurist, P.O. Box 30369, Bethesda Branch, Washington, D.C. 20014

The Gerontologist, 1 Dupont Circle, Washington, D.C. 20036

Goodyear Publishing Company, 15115 Sunset Boulevard, Pacific Palisades, Calif. 90272

Grosset & Dunlap, 51 Madison Avenue, New York, N.Y. 10010

Harcourt Brace Jovanovich, 757 Third Avenue, New York, N.Y. 10017

Harper's Magazine, 2 Park Avenue, New York, N.Y. 10016

The Humanist, 923 Kensington Avenue, Buffalo, N.Y. 14215

Johns Hopkins Press, Baltimore, Md. 21218

Journal of Comparative Family Studies, Department of Sociology, The University of Calgary, 2920 Twenty-fourth Avenue N.W., Calgary, Alberta, Canada T2N 1N4

Journal of Jewish Communal Service, 14 East Twenty-sixth Street, New York, N.Y. 10010

Journal of Marriage and the Family, 1219 University Avenue, S.E., Minneapolis, Minn. 55414

The Journal of Pastoral Care, 475 Riverside Drive, Suite 450, New York, N.Y. 10027

Little, Brown and Company, 34 Beacon Street, Boston, Mass. 02106

Macmillan Publishing Company, 866 Third Avenue, New York, N.Y. 10022

McCalls Magazine, 230 Park Avenue, New York, N.Y. 10017

David McKay Company, 750 Third Avenue, New York, N.Y. 10017

MH, 1800 North Kent Street, Rosslyn, Arlington, Va. 22209

National Council on Family Relations, 1219 University Avenue, S.E., Minneapolis, Minn. 55414

New Press, 30 Lesmill Road, Don Mills, Ontario, Canada

W. W. Norton & Company, 500 Fifth Avenue, New York, N.Y. 10036

Oxford University Press, 200 Madison Avenue, New York, N.Y. 10016

Pantheon Books, 201 East Fiftieth Street, New York, N.Y. 10022

Parents Magazine, 52 Vanderbilt Avenue, New York, N.Y. 10017

Prentice-Hall, Route 9W, Englewood Cliffs, N.J. 07632

Psychiatry, 1610 New Hampshire Avenue, N.W., Washington, D.C. 20009

Psychology Today, 1 Park Avenue, New York, N.Y. 10016

Public Affairs Pamphlets, 381 Park Avenue South, New York, N.Y. 10016

Random House, 201 East Fiftieth Street, New York, N.Y. 10022

Redbook Magazine, 230 Park Avenue, New York, N.Y. 10017

Science and Behavior Books, P.O. Box 11457, Palo Alto, Calif. 94306

Charles Scribner's Sons, 597 Fifth Avenue, New York, N.Y. 10017

Simon and Schuster, 630 Fifth Avenue, New York, N.Y. 10020

Smith College Studies in Social Work, Smith College School for Social Work, Northampton, Mass. 01060

Social Casework, 44 East Twenty-third Street, New York, N.Y. 10010

Social Problems, 114 Rockwell Hall, State University College, 1300 Elmwood Avenue, Buffalo, N.Y. 14222

Social Service Review, The University of Chicago Press, 5801 Ellis Avenue, Chicago, Ill. 60637

Social Work, 2 Park Avenue, New York, N.Y. 10016

U.S. Government Printing Office, Washington, D.C. 20402

Walker and Company, 720 Fifth Avenue, New York, N.Y. 10019

World Publishing Company, 2080 West 117th Street, Cleveland, Ohio 44111

Peter H. Wyden, 750 Third Avenue, New York, N.Y. 10017